Answered by Fire

Answered by Fire

The Cane Ridge Revival Reconsidered

LEONARD ALLEN and
CARISSE MICKEY BERRYHILL
Editors

Abilene Christian University Press

ANSWERED BY FIRE

The Cane Ridge Revival Reconsidered

ACU PRESS

ISBN 978-1-68426-351-6

Printed in the United States of America

Library of Congress Cataloging in Publication Data is on file at the Library of Congress, Washington, DC.

Scripture quotations are the author's own translation.

Cover design by Rick Gibson
Interior text design by Sandy Armstrong, Strong Design

For information contact:
Abilene Christian University Press
ACU Box 29138
Abilene, Texas 79699

1-877-816-4455
www.acupressbooks.com

26 / 7 6 5 4 3

Contents

PART III
Reconsidering Cane Ridge

Introduction

CARISSE MICKEY BERRYHILL

The 2019 Carroll Ellis Symposium, "America's Greatest Revival: Cane Ridge Reconsidered," was held August 13, 2019, at the Hillsboro Church of Christ in Nashville, Tennessee, hosted by Scott Sager of the Office of Church Services at Lipscomb University, and supported by a generous gift from Dr. David and Sherry Thomas. The event coincided with the 218th anniversary week of the great Cane Ridge meeting led by Barton W. Stone from August 6th to 12th, 1801, in Bourbon County, Kentucky, at the meeting house of the Presbyterian congregation he served at Cane Ridge.

The Cane Ridge revival can be considered the remarkable beginning of a reform movement in American Protestantism that under the initial leadership of Stone, Thomas and Alexander Campbell, and Walter Scott grew rapidly in the nineteenth and twentieth centuries. The Cane Ridge meeting attracted thousands of participants and observers from a wide variety of Christian groups. Despite their differences, participants joined in fasting, prayer, singing, and preaching to seek repentance and renewal, compelled by a unifying sense of divine presence and awed by manifestations of the power of the Spirit of God. Yet, for the most part, the experiential narratives of this and similar revivals during the Second Great Awakening in America have not persisted in Churches of Christ, which have for nearly two centuries emphasized cognitive apprehension of the biblical message, conformity to scriptural examples in matters of church life, and obedience to the ethical demands of the New Testament.

To examine the events of Cane Ridge and reconsider why its emphasis on the Holy Spirit faded, four Tennessee scholars of the Stone-Campbell movement convened to discuss Cane Ridge in a single-day format of nine short speeches arranged in three groups. Each group of three speeches was followed by a question-and-answer period.

The participating historians were C. Leonard Allen, whose main concern has been the importance of trinitarian life for Churches of Christ; James L. Gorman, who has examined the roots of the Churches of Christ in the evangelical Awakenings in Europe and America; John Mark Hicks, whose works on baptism and the Lord's Supper consider the experience of the Spirit in the body of Christ; and Richard T. Hughes, whose studies of Barton Stone point to sources of countercultural themes in Churches of Christ.

The symposium's impulse to look back to Cane Ridge is rooted in an ongoing reconsideration of the doctrine of the Trinity, evoked by challenges to established consensus in the Churches of Christ coming out of the cultural upheavals of the 1960s. These challenges included the charismatic movement, the civil rights movement, and the feminist movement. Participants' studies of the intellectual history of Churches of Christ have described the mid-twentieth-century shift in the hermeneutical and cultural thought of the churches. They have called for the recovery of a countercultural and mission-focused Christianity disentangled from American exceptionalism, from white supremacist hegemony, and from religious tribalism. Their attention to the scriptural narrative of the divine kingdom calls the church to affirm the redemptive purpose of God for all creation.

However, voices were missing at the 2019 Ellis Symposium. No female or black scholars were on the panel, even though the participation of women and blacks at Cane Ridge was detailed and the impact of the revival on attitudes toward slavery was featured. This event featuring scholarly appraisal of the Cane Ridge meeting would have benefitted from the diversity that had characterized the Cane Ridge meeting in the first place, and by doing so would have better embodied its spirit of unity.

Cane Ridge in Context

The first group of essays, "Cane Ridge in Context," describes the event, its predecessors, and its leaders. James Gorman's "Glorious Days" frames Cane Ridge as part of the inauguration of the Second Great Awakening, namely the Great Revival in the West spearheaded by James McGready and Barton W. Stone in Kentucky. Gorman outlines the political, social, and theological contexts of the Western revivals. Richard Hughes's "Champion of Christian Freedom" explores the radical spiritual freedom of the churches led by Stone from about 1803 to 1823, a freedom that eschewed creeds and organizations, even the earthly republic whose democratizing impulse underlay their movement, in favor of the liberty to opt in to the promises of salvation. Gorman's "Answered by Fire" details seven happenings at Cane Ridge, focusing on the "spiritual exercises," such as holy singing and falling, which imbued the meeting with awe.

Exploring Cane Ridge

Having described the meeting and its precedents, the second group of essays, "Exploring Cane Ridge," focuses closely on particular aspects of the meeting. John Mark Hicks's "Cane Ridge as a Communion Festival" connects Cane Ridge to a long tradition of Scots-Irish Presbyterian annual sacramental festivals characterized by fasting and repentance before the day of communion, followed by a day of thanksgiving. Richard Hughes in "Barton Stone, Cane Ridge, and Slavery" traces the development of Stone's thought on chattel slavery from 1797 to the end of his life, noting that the Cane Ridge meeting catalyzed Stone's own decision to free the slaves his marriage had brought him. The third essay, Gorman's "The Reproof of a Weak Woman," attends closely to accounts of women, black people, and children who exhorted participants to repent and receive conversion.

Reconsidering Cane Ridge

The final group of three essays, "Reconsidering Cane Ridge," ponders the spiritual legacy of Cane Ridge for today's churches. Leonard Allen's "Was Cane Ridge America's Pentecost?" takes up a dialogue with Paul Conkin's book *Cane Ridge: America's Pentecost* to assess the long-term impact of the meeting on American evangelical pietism and on the Stoneite legacy. Hicks, in "Revivalism, the Holy Spirit, and Unity," meditating on the unity experienced at Cane Ridge, recommends five "modes of visible unity" empowered today by the Spirit in the church. Allen's "Eclipse of Cane Ridge" describes how the radical freedom and unity of Cane Ridge were superseded by Alexander Campbell's emphasis on the "ancient order of things" and "ancient gospel" or plan of salvation. Allen asserts that in the crisis of postmodern Christianity, Cane Ridge can bear new witness "to the fresh, surprising, and sometimes strange work of God the Spirit" empowering churches "to live on God's mission."

This volume, like Anthony Dunnavant's *Cane Ridge in Context* (1992), takes a deeper look at a seminal event of the Second Great Awakening in America and ponders its meaning for its heirs today. It preserves the authors' 2019 presentations for wider distribution. Although it does not record the question and answer sessions, this volume provides something not available in the oral presentations: documentation of sources used by the presenters, including scattered eye-witness accounts of Cane Ridge and other revivals, as well as scholarly interpretations. It also includes an appendix containing seven lengthy excerpts from accounts by participants in the revival with questions for engagement.

The agonies of 2020 have reminded us again and again that failures of justice, health, and community oppress men, women, and children of every nation, tribe, and tongue around the globe. In the face of strife and separation, we turn our gaze back to the great gathering of 1801—and, yes, to Pentecost so long ago—and yearn for the communion that we see there and that we hope for in God's future. In such a time, our yearning rises as a common bond. Even when so much is lost, if we have eyes to see it and faith to follow, the Spirit is already at work renewing our mission to live out the love of God as one people.

PART I

CANE RIDGE IN CONTEXT

CHAPTER ONE

"Glorious Days of the Outpouring of the Spirit of God"

The Second Great Awakening

JAMES L. GORMAN

The Reverend James McGready (1758–1817) is widely acknowledged as the leader of the Second Great Awakening revivals in Kentucky. McGready described the revivals as "glorious days of the outpouring of the Spirit of God." He had witnessed three of these special times. He first witnessed God's Spirit outpoured in 1786 at a Sunday morning communion gathering in Pennsylvania—at that time, he experienced new birth conversion at the age of twenty-eight.[1] The second glorious day of God's outpoured Spirit was in 1789 during a series of revivals in Virginia and North Carolina that lasted into the early 1790s.[2] In fact, at one of these revivals (1791), McGready preached to a crowd that included Barton Stone when Stone was a student in North Carolina. After hearing McGready's persuasive sermon, Stone decided to seek religion.[3]

McGready described the third outpouring of God's Spirit in the revivals he led in Logan County, Kentucky, from 1797 to 1802—revivals that mark the beginning of the Second Great Awakening.[4] McGready had migrated westward in 1796 to Kentucky, where he pastored three congregations in Logan County. He immediately prepared his churches for a revival like those he experienced in the east. He had members of his congregations pray, fast, and participate in four-day sacramental occasions that had already become fertile ground for Presbyterian revivals, first in Scotland and then in America.[5] Starting in 1797 and culminating in 1801, McGready's region experienced massive revivals, while he published narratives of the revivals that made him famous. For example, the renowned Methodist leader Francis Asbury said in 1801 that if he were too tired or ill to preach, he could read McGready's accounts of the Logan County revival and have more effect on the crowd than with his own sermon.[6]

McGready's story reveals several themes, but most importantly, his description of the revivals is how the revivalists understood the early Second Great Awakening: "glorious days of the outpouring of the Spirit of God."

Definitions

In this opening chapter, I will cover in broad strokes several historical contexts of the Second Great Awakening in general and Cane Ridge in particular. But first I will provide two definitions.

First, the most basic definition of an awakening is a time of religious revival when people are awakened to their sinfulness and experience conversion. But awakenings are times of revitalization not only for individuals—they also revitalize churches and society. In this sense, awakenings are in some way responses to political, social, economic, and theological realities or crises.[7]

Second, historians debate when the First Great Awakening ended and when the Second began. The 1730s and 1740s saw the most intense period of revivals in the First Awakening, but evangelicals led revivals before that time, in the 1720s, and after that time—in fact, revivals continued into the 1790s.[8] So the timeline gets confusing because revivals never stopped between the two Awakenings. Nonetheless, most historians think of the Second Great Awakening as a nationwide series of revivals from the 1790s to the 1830s with three geographic centers of origin that contained bursts of revival activity: the Great Revival in the West (1797–1805), which is the context of Cane Ridge; the New England revivals (1790s to the early 1800s), centered at Yale; and New York revivals (1820s–1830s), whose major leader was Charles Grandison Finney.[9]

Beyond the revivals themselves, a massive movement for social reform also marked the Second Great Awakening. Christians of all stripes worked together in voluntary societies that printed Bibles and tracts, organized missions, and fought against slavery, drunkenness, and other social ills they believed were out of sync with a Christian society. However, the revivals and societies for social reform did not always include the same individuals. In fact, some of the more sectarian revivalists were wary of optimistic schemes to Christianize culture and opposed the reform societies.[10]

The Political Context

The revivals and reform movement occurred in a unique period of American history. I find at least three intertwined contexts especially significant for illuminating the Great Revival in the West. First, the political context of the 1780s saw the formation of the new nation's government, which led to heightened rhetoric of liberty, "unalienable rights" of all people, and democracy. The idea that all individuals were endowed with common sense to do everything from read the Bible to choose their political leaders influenced the democratization of American Christianity. This democratization often made Christians suspicious of authorities and any kind of elitism.[11] Furthermore, the disestablishment of religion created a religious marketplace that resulted in both competition and anxiety, as no one knew what to expect from this political-religious experiment.

The Social Context

Second, the social context was a growing population and steady western migration. People formed new settlements and pushed the frontier line further and further westward. Past historians under the spell of Frederick Jackson Turner's (1861–1932) frontier thesis almost personified the frontier: it was like an active agent drastically shaping all who entered its realm. Turner perceptively argued that the frontier environment influenced much of frontier life—independent character, love of simplicity and elimination of non-essentials, anti-clericalism, and love of democratic institutions.[12]

Certainly, the frontier context was important for early Presbyterian revivalists like James McGready and Barton Stone. In often sparsely populated areas, the annual communion gatherings that began on Friday and ended on Monday were infused with expectation as people came together to enact the rituals meant to lead people to awakening—fasting, prayer, impassioned preaching, and the Lord's Supper.[13] But the frontier context should not be overplayed. First, all the Kentucky revivalists were trained in the east and many had experienced similar revivals in the east. Second, camp meeting revivals like those on the frontier became common all over the United States by the 1810s.[14]

The social context also included the first major conversion of enslaved black people to Christianity. A trickle of African American converts began in the First Awakening, but the Second saw a major increase. Historians have identified reasons for the increase at this time. Scholars debate the significance of the continuity between evangelical revivalism and West African religious practices, but similarities such as rebirth at initiation and ecstatic bodily exercises may have made evangelicalism compelling to enslaved Africans. Also, evangelicals in the 1780s and 1790s were some of the fiercest abolitionists, sometimes freeing people they enslaved and condemning slavery as satanic. Furthermore, evangelical new birth theology, which suggested all converts were spiritually equal before God, could work to subvert the racial hierarchy and logic of racial slavery. These and other factors led to an increasing number of enslaved people embracing evangelical Christianity during the Second Great Awakening and a consequent biracial evangelical revivalism that deeply shaped both black and white religious cultures in American Christianity.[15]

The Theological Context

Third, the theological context of the Great Revival in the West emphasized the new birth conversion experience. Although the Presbyterian revivals of the early Second Great Awakening were exciting times to gather for preaching, singing, fellowship, and communion, all the evangelical revivals, whether Presbyterian, Baptist, or Methodist, had one ever-present aim: to procure new birth conversions. In the evangelical tradition of McGready and Stone, revivals created space for the "outpouring of God's Spirit," and that outpouring was most clearly manifested in God's work of "new birth" conversion.

New Birth Conversion

New birth was the moment in time when God changed a person's corrupt nature and saved them from eternity in hell. Perhaps the most influential articulation of new birth theology was George

Whitefield's 1737 sermon *The Nature and Necessity of Our New Birth in Christ Jesus*, which went through more than twenty editions in the American colonies and Britain.[16] The sermon exemplified the evangelical understanding of "new birth" conversion during both Awakenings.[17] Whitefield argued that "regeneration" or "new birth" in Christ Jesus was the "Hinge on which the Salvation of each of us turns" and a point on which "all *sincere* Christians, of whatever Denomination, agree."[18] Whitefield argued that no one could be saved without the spiritual cleansing of new birth because that was when the Holy Spirit purified the soul's corrupt nature. Unconverted people could seek inward new birth by using the "instituted means of grace," such as fasting, prayer, hearing and reading Scripture, and receiving communion, to move toward "experimentally" (i.e., experientially) knowing the Holy Spirit.[19] The revivalists used all these means of grace to move people toward the Spirit's converting act.

James McGready's two volumes of sermons make clear that he had new birth conversion at the center of his revival preaching and understanding of the Christian life.[20] McGready urged hearers to examine themselves thoroughly and ask, "Have I experienced new birth?" That was the first question God would ask them on judgment day.[21] McGready hoped that by persistently urging sinners to examine themselves he would incite conviction or awakening—terms he often used interchangeably. His sermons were tools to convict unregenerated people; his preaching sought to jolt them into seeing their sinful nature and doomed eternity. For example, Barton Stone explained McGready's preaching like this:

> His coarse tremulous voice excited in me the idea of something unearthly. . . . Every thing appeared by him forgotten, but the salvation of souls. Such earnestness—such zeal—such powerful persuasion, enforced

> by the joys of heaven and miseries of hell, I had never witnessed before. My mind was chained by him, and followed him closely in his rounds of heaven, earth, and hell, with feelings indescribable. His concluding remarks were addressed to the sinner to flee the wrath to come without delay. Never before had I comparatively felt the force of truth. Such was my excitement, that had I been standing, I should have probably sunk to the floor under the impression.[22]

Historians also identify a major theological change in the conception of new birth in the Second Awakening. Evangelists in the First Awakening typically emphasized God's decision and timing in conversion, whereas those in the Second tended to place the decision in the hands of the seeker. The First Awakening expected long seasons of seeking conversion, whereas the Second saw shorter and shorter periods of seeking.

Stone on the New Birth

For one example of these theological changes, in 1804 Barton Stone defined new birth as God's gracious gift in response to a person's belief in the gospel. Stone retained the experiential aspect of new birth—God effected a substantial, supernatural change in the individual. But Stone changed the order of the new birth process. He argued that a person's belief in the testimony of the gospel prompted God to give the believer new birth conversion immediately.[23] Stone rejected traditional views of predestination and election, advocating free will, or what historians call "Arminianism." In fact, this theology of new birth was one of the major causes of his break from the Presbyterians.[24]

Stone's theological development reflected larger trends in American history—the political and social environment had raised up the individual as supreme and the individual's freedom to choose as a basic human right. Even in the preaching of an orthodox Calvinist like James McGready, new birth theology seemed to emphasize free will.[25] Populism, individualism, and anti-authoritarianism combined in the early national period to create one of the most active periods of religious change in American history. A broad Arminian shift in conversion theology was one of those changes.[26]

Two Key Effects

It is hard to overestimate the influence of the new birth conversion experience in shaping the Second Great Awakening. I will highlight two key effects. First, new birth provided a basis for interdenominational cooperation because evangelicals deemphasized denominational creeds and confessions, pointing instead to the new birth conversion experience as the essential marker of Christian identity. That is, those who experienced conversion were true Christians and could thus share pulpits and communion. Denominational affiliation was no longer the key criterion of fellowship.

But new birth was a double-edged sword when it came to Christian unity, for even as it created a foundation for interdenominational cooperation, its clear demarcation of Christian and non-Christian based on a subjective individual experience hardened division. For example, revivalist Gilbert Tennett earned notoriety in the First Awakening by preaching about the dangers of unconverted ministers, essentially telling Christians to leave congregations if their preacher had not given testimony that he had experienced new birth conversion.[27]

Second, new birth theology implied a radical egalitarian message of spiritual equality. If all who experienced new birth were spiritually equal in the eyes of God, then doors suddenly opened to challenge or momentarily transcend any construct that had created a hierarchy between people. In other words, some evangelicals used the spiritual equality founded on new birth theology to challenge gender hierarchies (e.g., women took a more active role), racial hierarchies (e.g., enslaved and free black people become more active), and even children got involved.

"The Declension of Vital Piety"

Another aspect of the theological context includes an apparent crisis. Like the First Awakening, the Second Awakening began amid a perceived religious decline and cultural breakdown.[28] Historians debate whether the historical situation was accurately reflected in the ministers' narratives of decline, but concern about decline permeates the primary sources. For example, Stone began his history of Christians with this crisis: "Towards the close of the eighteenth century, there was an unusual dearth in the professors of religion, throughout the western country, both among the preachers and the people. In the commencement of the present century, the more pious became seriously alarmed at the prevalence of vice and the declension of vital piety." Many ministerial accounts of the revivals began with the assertion that religiosity had declined. Ministers often cited this decline as the reason they had their congregations fasting and praying for a revival. As revivalists used all the instituted means of grace to incite revival amid a perceived decline in piety, God "*answered by fire*; for he poured out his spirit in ways almost miraculous."[29]

Conclusion

Historians have always had much to consider when reflecting on the causes of the Second Great Awakening. It is not difficult to see the many ways the Second Great Awakening was a response to the political, social, and theological upheaval of the early national era of United States history. It is undeniable that the revivals revitalized individuals, churches, and culture. Of course, if we ask the revivalists who left accounts of these events about the causes of the revival, it becomes clear they were convinced the only reasonable explanation was that they lived in an extraordinary time of the outpouring of the Spirit of God.

NOTES

[1] M'Gready, *Posthumous Works*, 1:40.

[2] M'Gready, *Posthumous Works*, 1:40.

[3] Stone, *Biography*, 8–9.

[4] M'Gready, *Posthumous Works*, 1:40.

[5] Schmidt, *Holy Fairs*; Conkin, *Cane Ridge*, 54–63.

[6] Conkin, *Cane Ridge*, 55–56; Asbury, *The Journal of the Rev. Francis Asbury*, 3:12, 15, 24.

[7] Price, "Great Awakening(s)," 2:913, 920–21.

[8] The best treatment of the Great Awakening is by Kidd, *The Great Awakening*.

[9] Carroll, *The Routledge Historical Atlas of Religion in America*, 62–63.

[10] For more information, see Moore and Calhoon, "Evangelicals: Nineteenth Century," 2:800; Brekus, *Strangers and Pilgrim*, 122–23; McClymond, "Christian Revival and Renewal Movements," 244–62.

[11] Hatch, *The Democratization of American Christianity*.

[12] According to Turner's 1893 essay and subsequent theory, free land, westward expansion, and the continual process of beginning again on the line of settlement explain the development of American democratic life and character. See Turner, "The Significance of the Frontier," 1–38.

[13] Methodists did conduct camp meetings in the late 1780s, but the Presbyterian sacramental occasions influenced their rise to national prominence, according to Gaustad and Barlow. Camp meetings eventually became institutionalized, especially by the Methodists. Baptists and Presbyterians moved away from camp meeting religion. Both groups more than the Methodists critiqued the emotionalism of the meetings and had more constituents who rejected the Arminian theology of these revivals, according to Dickson. However, the Stone Christians did continue the tradition of sacramental occasions as revivals into at least the late 1820s. Gaustad, Barlow, and Dishno, *New Historical Atlas*, 333; Bruce, "Camp Meetings," 1:348; T. Allen, "REVIVALS," 140–41.

[14] For areas of camp meeting strength, see Boles, *The Great Revival*, xix.

[15] Gorman, "Evangelical Revivalism and Race Relations," 21–38.

[16] Mahaffey, *The Accidental Revolutionary*, 264.

[17] Cohen, "Great Awakening," 4:38.

[18] Whitefield, *The Nature and Necessity*, 1.

[19] Whitefield, *The Nature and Necessity*, 11.

[20] Nearly all of McGready's extant sermons focused on conversion. Contemporary reports suggest that this was his normal content. See Scott, "James McGready: Son of Thunder," 49–61; M'Gready, *Posthumous Works*, 1:iv, vii; Stone, "A Short History," 54; Opie, "James McGready: Theologian of Frontier Revivalism," 450. For this section, I draw especially from two sermons, both titled "The New Birth." See 2:68–95, 96–118.

[21] M'Gready, *Posthumous Works*, 2:71.

[22] Rogers and Stone, "A Short History," 121.

[23] Stone, "A Compendious View of the Gospel," 191–221.

[24] For these developments see Williams, *Barton Stone: A Spiritual Biography*, 79–94.

[25] For example, see M'Gready, *Posthumous Works*, 1:47–49, 229; M'Gready, *Posthumous Works*, 2:187–96, 105, 116–18.

[26] Historians use the terms Arminianism and Calvinism to represent the ideas of free will and predestination. Arminianism centers on free will. Free will means that God equips all people with the ability to choose or reject Christ, to believe or not believe; God did not predestine each individual's eternity. Calvinism centers on divine predestination. Divine predestination consists of both divine election to heaven and divine reprobation to hell. For fuller definitions of the way I am using these two terms, see Thuesen, *Predestination*, 220, 224.

[27] Tennent, "The Danger of an Unconverted Ministry," 87–93.

[28] Brekus, *Strangers and Pilgrims*, 34; Boles, *The Great Revival*, 12–24.

[29] Stone, "History of the Christian Church. No. I," 74.

CHAPTER TWO

The Champion of Christian Freedom and the Cane Ridge Revival

RICHARD T. HUGHES

From their rational reading of the biblical text to their legacy of debating to their claim that the Holy Spirit is confined to the biblical text and speaks to us only through rational argument, Churches of Christ have been shaped and formed by the highly rational mind of Alexander Campbell who was, in turn, deeply indebted to the eighteenth-century Enlightenment—the Age of Reason.

But Churches of Christ are heirs to another impulse as well, one that today seems quaint and almost out of place for most of the history of this tradition. This second impulse has more in common with modern Pentecostalism than it does with modern Churches of Christ for it opens itself to the free and mysterious work of the Holy Spirit—which could cause a man, woman, or child to run, jerk, laugh, bark, fall, and perhaps even speak in unknown tongues.

This second impulse is the legacy of Barton W. Stone, the man who shaped our tradition in important ways for some twenty-two years—from 1801, the year of the Cane Ridge Revival, to 1823 when Alexander Campbell debated W. L. McCalla in Washington, Kentucky. By 1823, the Stoneites in Kentucky were committed to little more than freedom in Christ through the power of the Holy Spirit. They had no church organization to speak of. They had never heard of "the five-step plan of salvation" or the "five acts of worship" or any other formalized structures that might constrain them. And they refused to insist on baptism for entry into the church. They rejoiced in the liberty with which God had set them free and lived in the power of the Spirit that assured them of their salvation.

Champion of Christian Freedom

For Stone and his followers, Christian freedom meant above all else the freedom of ordinary men and women to reject the religious pronouncements of popes, priests, bishops, and clerics of every kind. Instead, the Stoneites—unlettered as they were—claimed the right to search the Bible for themselves and draw their own conclusions regarding the truths of the Christian faith. One of Stone's followers, for example, built his case on the well-known phrase in the *Declaration of Independence*, "certain inalienable rights," but refocused that phrase to claim the inalienable right of "free investigation, [and] sober and diligent inquiry after [religious] truth."[1]

John Rogers, a well-known preacher in both the Stone and Campbell sides of the movement, eloquently described the freedom to search for truth to which the Stoneites were committed:

> The fatal error of all reformers has been that they have too hastily concluded *that they knew the whole truth, and have settled back upon the same principles of proscription, intolerance and persecution, against which they so strongly remonstrated*. . . . Having, then, full in our view, this fatal rock, on which so many reformers have split, may we studiously avoid it. We have no reason to conclude, we know all the truth. . . . We have nothing to lose in this inquiry after truth. We have no system to bind us to human opinions.[2]

It seems clear that the Christian freedom the Stoneites claimed was reinforced by the civic freedom they enjoyed in the new American nation. One Stoneite wrote, for example, that "the present conflict between the Bible and party creeds and confessions . . . is perfectly analogous to the revolutionary war between Britain and America; liberty was contended for on the one side, and dominion and power on the other."[3]

But we have not yet grasped the truly radical nature of the Stoneites' commitment to freedom. For theirs was a freedom to stand against the very civic order—the very American nation—that in so many ways inspired them. Christian freedom for them meant freedom to serve the kingdom of God that elevated impoverished and marginalized people, including enslaved people, and to reject the principalities and powers that elevated the wealthy, the privileged, and the politically connected.

Freedom for Stone meant freedom to serve "the least of these," regardless of popular standards of decorum and respectability. "No Christian lives for himself," he wrote. "Not self but the Lord is the great end of his living. . . . Like an obedient servant, he says, Lord what wilt thou have me to do? And when that will is known, he flies to do [it], not regarding how great the sacrifice of wealth, ease, or reputation."[4] Stone offered a statement in 1841 that expressed that conviction as well as anything he ever wrote, though that same conviction characterized his entire career. "You must not mind earthly things," he wrote, "nor set your affections on them—not to be conformed to the world . . . . Here you have no abiding place, but are as strangers and pilgrims seeking a better country."[5]

That better country was the kingdom of God that, Stone believed, would one day triumph over all the earth, subverting every human government, including that of the United States. Accordingly, he wrote,

> The lawful King, Jesus Christ, will shortly put them [human governments] all down, and reign with his Saints on earth a thousand years, without a rival. . . . Then shall all man made laws and governments be burnt up forever. These are the seat of the beast. . . . Christians have no right to make laws and governments for themselves . . . [and] all should submit to the government and laws of our King. . . . We must cease to support any other government on earth by our counsels, co-operation, and choice.[6]

In line with that conviction, the Stoneites refused to vote or hold political office and rejected the laws of the United States pertaining to American slavery.

But the radical freedom that defined the Stoneite movement for twenty-two years—from the Cane Ridge Revival to 1823 when they heard Alexander Campbell preach for the very first time—also left them longing for some sort of structure, for something more concrete to which they could tether themselves and their churches. And structure is precisely what Campbell offered when he debated the Presbyterian preacher, W. L. McCalla, in

Washington, Kentucky, in 1823. The topic of that debate? The proper subjects and the proper mode of baptism.

In that very same year, 1823, Campbell launched *The Christian Baptist*, a journal widely read by the followers of Barton Stone. By 1825, the name "Alexander Campbell" was well known in Kentucky. He began his series "A Restoration of the Ancient Order of Things" in *The Christian Baptist,* in which he defined in minute detail the proper structure, organization, and practice of the primitive church. The die was cast: Campbell increasingly would become the dominant influence among the Stoneites in Kentucky and, indeed, among Churches of Christ, and Barton W. Stone would increasingly become our movement's "forgotten man."

Liberated by the Kentucky Revivals

Our question today, then, is this: Who was this Barton W. Stone? Who was this man who proclaimed freedom for Christians through the power of the Holy Spirit? There is no way to understand Stone and his theology apart from the great Cane Ridge Revival of 1801 which he helped to lead. And there is no way to understand why he found that event so compelling, so inspiring, and so transformative apart from an oppressive form of Calvinism that dominated the thinking of so many Christians on the American frontier, including Barton W. Stone.

Prior to the Great Revival, he confessed, "I . . . believed, and taught, that mankind were so totally depraved that they could do nothing acceptable to God, till his Spirit, by some physical, almighty, and mysterious power had quickened, enlightened, and regenerated the heart." Under such a system, the sinner, he said, "must be damned." There was no exit, no escape from the fires of eternal hell unless, perchance, God chose that particular sinner for salvation. These doctrines, Stone wrote, "were as mountains pressing me down to the shades of death." His mind, he said, was lost "in gloom . . . and all my joys were gone."[7]

One Stoneite—B. F. Hall—offered a revealing glimpse into the traumatic spiritual struggles many experienced when under the influence of the version of Calvinism so popular on the American frontier. Hall told that when he was only seventeen-years-old, he sought God "back of the field, near a hollow, in a briar thicket. . . . I knelt for some moments in silence, for words came not to my lips. I could think of nothing to say. My pent-up grief was intence [*sic*]. . . . Tears gushed unbidden from my eyes. I sobbed aloud."[8]

These were the kinds of experiences that pushed Barton Stone into the biblical text, searching for some relief, for some word of grace, for an exit, for an escape from certain damnation. And he found that exit in John 20:31: "These are written, that ye might believe that Jesus is the Christ, the Son of God, and that believing, ye might have life through his name." "This glimpse of faith—of truth," he wrote, "was the first divine ray of light, that ever led my distressed, perplexed mind from the labyrinth of Calvinism and error, in which I had so long been bewildered. It was that which led me into the rich pastures of gospel-liberty."[9]

It was that discovery of "gospel-liberty" that prepared Stone's mind for what he would hear and witness at a revival in Logan County, Kentucky, in 1801. There, Stone heard James McGready and other ministers preach a message very much like the gospel truths he had found in the biblical text. And the message preached on that occasion produced behavior unlike anything Stone had ever seen. "The scene to me," he said, "was new, and passing strange."

> It baffled description. Many, very many fell down, as men slain in battle, and continued for hours together in an apparently breathless and motionless state—sometimes for a few moments reviving, and exhibiting

> symptoms of life by a deep groan, or piercing shriek, or by a prayer for mercy most fervently uttered.[10]

What Stone said next is crucial. Recall that in earlier times, Stone believed "that mankind were so totally depraved that they could do nothing acceptable to God, till his Spirit, by some physical, almighty, and mysterious power had quickened, enlightened, and regenerated the heart." The problem was that God enlivened the bodies and enlightened the hearts only of those few whom he called and elected for salvation. The rest were doomed to damnation.

But here in Logan County, Kentucky, Stone witnessed spiritual and physical release, deliverance, and salvation on the part of all who heard and all who believed. After falling down "as men slain in battle," Stone wrote, and "after lying thus for hours, they obtained deliverance." And by "they," Stone meant all of them, every single one who heard the gospel proclaimed and believed on the Lord Jesus Christ. Thus, he wrote:

> The gloomy cloud, which had covered their faces, seemed gradually and visibly to disappear, and hope in smiles brightened into joy—they would rise shouting deliverance, and then would address the surrounding multitude in language truly eloquent and impressive. With astonishment did I hear men, women and children declaring the wonderful works of God, and the glorious mysteries of the gospel. Their appeals were solemn, heart-penetrating, bold, and free. Under such addresses many others would fall down into the same state from which the speakers had just been delivered.[11]

All this we must grasp if we hope to understand Barton Stone's relation to the great Cane Ridge Revival. For these were the things he saw and heard on the eve of that revival, and these were the ideas that transformed his preaching from Calvinist gloom and doom to what he often now described as "gospel-liberty."

"Like Fire in Dry Stubble"

Having left Logan County, Stone returned to his own congregation at Cane Ridge where he preached the following Lord's Day. And he took for his text that Sunday Mark 16:15–16: "Go ye into all the world and preach the gospel to every creature. He that believeth and is baptized shall be saved, and he that believeth not shall be damned." Here was a text that turned Calvinism upside down. For Stone found in this text substantial evidence that the gospel call was for every human being, not just for the elect.

Accordingly, Stone wrote, "On the universality of the gospel, and faith as the condition of salvation, [my sermon] principally dwelt, and [I] urged the sinner to believe now, and be saved." Many found Stone's message liberating beyond words, were moved to tears, and "returned home weeping."[12]

Just a few days later, Stone preached at the other congregation he served, a church in Concord, Kentucky, and delivered the very same message of gospel freedom. The results were predictable. "In less than twenty minutes," Stone recalled, "scores had fallen to the ground—paleness, trembling, and anxiety appeared in all—some attempted to fly from the scene panic stricken, but they either fell, or returned immediately to the crowd, as unable to get away."[13]

"The effects of this meeting through the country," Stone wrote, "were like fire in dry stubble driven by a strong wind." Indeed, he soon held what he called "a protracted meeting at Concord" that lasted "five days and nights without ceasing." "The whole country appeared to be in motion to the place, and multitudes of all denominations attended."[14]

All these events led up to the great Cane Ridge Revival that began "on Thursday or Friday before the third Lord's-day in August, 1801."[15] By now, word of the liberating gospel of grace—the gospel that freed men and women from the constraints of Calvinism—had spread throughout the surrounding countryside. And thousands made their way to Cane Ridge.

Stone recalled that "the roads were literally crowded with wagons, carriages, horsemen, and footmen, moving to the solemn camp. . . . It was judged, by military men on the ground, that there were between twenty and thirty thousand [people] collected." Preachers from various denominations—Methodist, Baptist, and Presbyterian—converted wagons into pulpits and preached simultaneously in different parts of the clearing. And as Stone recalled, "We . . . all preached the same things—free salvation urged upon all by faith and repentance." The meeting continued for six or seven days" and "would have continued longer," Stone wrote, "but provisions for such a multitude failed in the neighborhood."[16]

Recall again that when laboring under the constraints of Calvinism, Stone fully believed that one could not be saved until God's "Spirit, by some physical, almighty, and mysterious power had quickened, enlightened, and regenerated the heart" of the one whom God had predestined for salvation. But now Stone believed that God willed the salvation of *all* humankind. And once again the proof of salvation lay in some physical demonstration of saving grace.

We should not be surprised, then, that the great Cane Ridge Revival, like the smaller revivals that preceded it, produced what Stone called bodily agitations or "exercises" that Stone described as "the falling exercise—the jerks—the dancing exercise—the barking exercise—the laughing and singing exercise, &c."[17] James Gorman explores those "exercises" in substantial detail in the following chapter.

If today we find these exercises somewhat quaint, if not bizarre, Stone viewed them as evidence of the power of the Spirit of God transforming human life. But Stone was convinced that the ultimate test of a transformed life was neither the jerks nor the barks but a life of radical discipleship. We shall explore this dimension of Barton Stone in Chapter Five, "Barton Stone, Cane Ridge, and Slavery."

NOTES

[1]Gregg and Gregg, "An Apology," 39–40.
[2]Rogers, "The Church of Christ at Concord," 258.
[3]Smith, "To the Editor of the Christian Messenger," 249.
[4]Stone, "Christian Expositor," 272.
[5]Stone, "Christian Union, Lecture III," 316–17.
[6]Stone, "Reflections of Old Age," 123–26.
[7]Stone, *Biography*, 32.
[8]Hall, "The Proud Preacher: The Autobiography of B. F. Hall."
[9]Stone, *Biography*, 33. See the Appendix.
[10]Stone, *Biography*, 34.
[11]Stone, *Biography*, 30–35.
[12]Stone, *Biography*, 36.
[13]Stone, *Biography*, 36–37.
[14]Stone, *Biography*, 37.
[15]Stone, *Biography*, 37.
[16]Stone, *Biography*, 37–38.
[17]Stone, *Biography*, 39.

CHAPTER THREE

"Answered by Fire"

What Really Happened at Cane Ridge?

JAMES L. GORMAN

"For a long time, I have wondered what really happened at Cane Ridge in 1801."[1] That's the first line of Paul Conkin's book *Cane Ridge: America's Pentecost*. I had the same question when forced to grapple with Cane Ridge for one of my Master of Divinity comprehensive exams at Abilene Christian University. In a case study assignment, I was Richard McNemar, one of the revivalists who worked with Barton Stone. My congregation was about to split because some believed the religious exercises at the revivals—falling, jerking, barking, and others—were inauthentic, whereas others believed they were a legitimate work of the Holy Spirit. How should I proceed? Thankfully for me then and for us now, Conkin's book provides a 170-page answer to the question: What really happened at Cane Ridge? I will rely on him throughout this chapter.

I will provide brief descriptions of seven things that happened at the Cane Ridge revival and then focus on the religious exercises that came to epitomize the Great Revival in the West.

Seven Happenings

The Cane Ridge sacramental gathering began on Friday, August 6, 1801, and continued sporadically until Thursday, August 12. Somewhere between 10,000 and more than 30,000 people experienced Cane Ridge on one or more days—all the estimates are questionable because eyewitnesses reported drastically different numbers.

In a list of things that happened, communion should be mentioned first, even though it was not administered until Sunday, the third day of the revival. But the key reason for the gathering was to take communion, as we will see further in Chapter Four. Annual gatherings for communion were a staple in the Presbyterian yearly calendar. In fact, in 1801 alone, at least fifty congregations in Kentucky held a four-day sacramental gathering—from Friday to Monday was the typical time.[2] The most reliable estimates of communicants at Cane Ridge range from 800 to 1,100.[3]

Second, people camped at Cane Ridge. As the communion gatherings grew in popularity, more people attended and traveled farther to be part of them. Meetings quickly outgrew local accommodations, so camping became necessary. Many of those who traveled long distances in wagons brought what they needed to camp. Barton Stone later recalled that "the roads were literally crowded with wagons, carriages, horsemen, and footmen moving to the solemn camp."[4] On Saturday, one attendee counted 147 wagons encamped on the Cane Ridge grounds.[5] Camping created a new kind of experience: imagine rural fields transforming into small cities. Camping at a meeting like Cane Ridge offered many of the same qualities of city life—anonymity, the opportunity to escape old roles and create new ones, and a chance to escape the concerns of daily life.[6] Camping also came with logistical challenges—unfortunately, none of the eyewitness accounts mention logistics, such as where people used the restroom. Cane Ridge was not the first camp meeting, but it became the most famous of the early camp meetings—and camp meeting religion became a major force in American Christianity.

Third, interdenominational fellowship happened at Cane Ridge. Evangelicals started working across denominational lines in the early eighteenth century. That interdenominational tradition culminated in the 1790s, as evangelicals joined hands across denominations for common tasks: missions and Bible societies were the most popular in those early days.[7] Although Methodists and Baptists had separately conducted revivals in the West in the 1790s, it was in 1800 that Methodists joined James McGready's Presbyterian revivals. That is why Paul Conkin marks 1800 as the beginning of an "ecumenical tradition."[8] But regardless of when the tradition began, the Cane Ridge revival was interdenominational not only in attendance but also in leadership—Methodists and Baptists preached and Methodists even participated in the planning.[9]

However, there were some limits to the early ecumenism at Cane Ridge. For example, although Methodists were welcome to take communion, and probably around 200 Methodists did take communion, only Presbyterian ministers presided at the communion tables. Baptists often did not take communion. Similarly, only certain ministers could preach from the two official platforms—the church building and the "tent," a covered lecture platform 100 yards from the meetinghouse. At least thirteen Presbyterian ministers and four Methodist ministers preached in the building or tent, but no one recorded Baptist ministers preaching from either place. One black Baptist minister preached to a separate gathering of black attendees, and the mention of Baptist ministers being present suggests that they exhorted at smaller gatherings.

Fourth, Cane Ridge witnessed biracial revivalism. Unfortunately, we know tantalizingly little about race relations at Cane Ridge. Sources mention that one of the four assembly areas at Cane Ridge was for black people, but no one left a detailed description of this black assembly. One eyewitness said white ministers did preach to the black assembly, and we have eyewitness accounts of at least one black minister preaching and black lay exhorters active in the black assembly. It is highly unlikely that black preachers addressed white assemblies. Based on the sparse primary source evidence about race relations at Cane Ridge and broader evangelical experiences, we can assume that the revival was, for the most part, spatially segregated.[10]

However, there is much more to the racial story of Cane Ridge than segregation. Many leading revivalists of the Great Revival in the West were committed abolitionists, and Cane Ridge was a hub of abolitionism. For example, Barton Stone filed manumission papers for people he enslaved (Ned and Lucy) in 1801, the same year as the Cane Ridge revival. Further, David Purviance, an elder at Cane Ridge, was elected in the 1790s to the Kentucky legislature as an antislavery representative. In 1800, the Cane Ridge congregation presented a resolution to the West Lexington Presbytery, stating that slavery was evil and slaveholders should be ejected from the Presbyterian Church. Leading Presbyterians in Kentucky such as David Rice had publicly opposed slavery as early as the 1790s. And these Presbyterian revivalists were not alone—leading Methodists, Baptists, and Congregationalists called slavery a satanic creation that could not be synced with Christianity. Paul Conkin wrote that "antislavery sentiment became almost synonymous with the [Great Revival in the West]." Indeed, Stone depicted the revival as an active emancipator when he wrote, "This revival cut the bonds of many poor slaves."[11]

Furthermore, the revivalists used the egalitarian implications of new birth conversion to make war on hierarchies and elitism of all types, including parts of the racial hierarchy that white people took for granted. For example, revivalist James McGready argued that "an ignorant negro, who had never learned his letters, but had embraced Christ, understands [the Bible] unspeakably better than the wisest man in an unregenerate state."[12] To be sure, white revivalists used language such as "poor negro" that betrayed their racist and paternalist views, but at the time of the Cane Ridge revival, evangelical revivalists such as Barton Stone were among an enslaved person's greatest allies. In 1801, many of the revivalists were still staunchly abolitionist, even if that would change in the next decade.

The biracial revivalism at Cane Ridge was, therefore, complex. New birth theology had a profound egalitarian effect on race relations. Some of the revivalists even envisioned the revivals as active emancipators, a sure sign of the coming millennial reign of Christ. Further, the new political ideology of "unalienable rights" suggested that involuntary slavery was unjust. With all this taken together, the Christian hope of all things being made right in the consummation of Christ's kingdom began looking less like a future reality and more like one coming to earth in the heat of God's outpoured Spirit in the revivals. Yet social structures and racial norms such as slavery and segregated space shaped the church and society in the opposite direction—revivalist egalitarianism remained primarily a spiritual equality rather than equality in society or even in churches. Rather than the beginning of racial unity, the Great Revival in the West catalyzed racial divisions in the church that mirrored the racialization of society.

Fifth, many people preached and exhorted throughout the revival. There were two centers of preaching activity in addition to the church building and the tent: a black assembly area about 150 yards southeast of the building and a fallen tree 15 feet off the ground located about 100 yards east of the meetinghouse.[13] There were also dozens of informal circles and prayer groups spread throughout the grounds. Barton Stone recalled four or five ministers preaching at the same time.[14] Sermons typically moved from a persuasive section to an exhortatory section with strong emotional appeals.[15] Hundreds of people, including women and children, also exhorted at the meeting.[16]

Sixth, attendees participated in the established religious practices of these revivals, including fasting, prayer, and singing. Fasting and prayer went hand in hand. Fasting represented individual and communal repentance and the giving up of worldliness, and in prayer the people called upon God to forgive their sins and to bring about a revival in their individual hearts and in their communities. Prayer and fasting were essential in times of religious crisis, and the perceived crisis of decline in religion animated the fast-day sermons and prayers at the beginning of the revival. Leaders who led congregations in fasting and prayer throughout the 1790s often explicitly called for God to pour out God's Spirit, to awaken the community, and to convert sinners.[17]

Many accounts of the revivals mention the singing that took place. The revival hymns "reduced doctrine to melodic and easily memorized lines."[18] The song leader often gave out a line and the congregation would respond in rhythm. In this way, large groups of people could learn new catchy songs quickly. In the earliest accounts of the revivals, people regularly linked the singing with the revival in general and religious exercises in particular.[19]

Seventh, people experienced new birth conversion—Stone estimated that between 500 and 1000 people experienced conversion at Cane Ridge.[20] The new birth conversion process followed a basic pattern: the sinner was awakened by a conviction of their sinfulness, which led first to a sense of dread and despair but then moved to a cathartic feeling of relief and joy, sometimes even to an ecstatic religious experience. This conversion process emerges in almost every eyewitness account of the religious exercises, but conversion was not *always* accompanied by religious exercises. And those who experienced religious exercises were not *always* undergoing conversion. Let's examine these exercises.

The Religious Exercises

An excerpt from Barton Stone's autobiography will guide our examination. Beyond considering the basics of the religious exercises, I will highlight the criteria Stone used to weigh the authenticity of the diverse exercises.[21]

The most common of all the exercises was falling. One minister who sought to keep an accurate count estimated that 3,000 people fell at Cane Ridge (but Conkin thinks the number was much lower).[22] Stone wrote, "The subject of this exercise would, generally, with a piercing scream, fall like a log on the floor, earth, or mud, and appear as dead." After hours and sometimes days, the person would eventually arise and begin witnessing about God's grace and exhorting all in earshot to repent of sins and seek conversion. Stone said this exercise happened to all ages and to both sinners and saints. He gave an example of two women who fell, and he pointed to their "almost superhuman" language and their subsequent commitment to the church to suggest the falling exercise was supernatural and for legitimate ends.[23]

When many people fell, it could become a safety hazard. For example, at the Cabin Creek sacrament in 1801, so many fell on the third night that they had to move the bodies to keep them from being crushed. Those fallen "were collected together and laid out in order, on two squares of the meeting-house; which, like so many dead corpses, covered a considerable part of the floor," according to Richard McNemar.[24] Camp meetings eventually prepared special places for those afflicted by exercises. For example, Benjamin Latrobe's 1809 sketch of a Methodist camp meeting revealed to the right of the camp "a boarded enclosure filled with straw, into which the converted were thrown that they might kick about without injuring themselves."[25]

Stone next described the jerks:

> Sometimes the subject of the jerks would be affected in some one member of the body, and sometimes in the whole system. When the head alone was affected, it would be jerked backward and forward, or from side to side. . . . When When the whole system was affected, I have seen the person stand in one place, and jerk backward and forward in quick succession, their head nearly touching the floor behind and before.[26]

Three pieces of evidence suggested to Stone that the jerks were from God. First, they happened to all classes of people, sinners and saints. Second, the jerks were involuntary. He had even seen wicked people affected, "and all the time cursing the jerks, while they were thrown to the earth with violence."[27] Third, he had never seen anyone with the jerks get hurt.

The dancing exercise usually began with the jerks. When the jerks ceased, only heavenly dancing remained. "The smile of heaven shone on the countenance of the subject, and assimilated to angels appeared the whole person," Stone recalled.[28]

The barking exercise was a pejorative name given because of the noise made when someone was affected by the jerks—so it was not really a separate exercise. Stone described: "A person affected with the jerks, especially in his head, would often make a grunt, or bark, if you please, from the suddenness of the jerk."[29]

The laughing exercise included "a loud, hearty laughter, but one *sui generis*; it excited laughter in none else. The subject appeared rapturously solemn, and his laughter excited solemnity in saints and sinners."[30] A very unnatural thing—solemnly laughing.

Stone describes the running exercise as something more like a person's attempt to get away from the exercises: when they felt the bodily agitations coming on, they would run to escape being affected. But the runners typically didn't get far before they fell. In the example Stone gave of running, the runner who fell and eventually experienced conversion became a "zealous member of the church," suggesting this was God's work.[31]

Finally, Stone described a singing exercise that was "more unaccountable than any thing else I ever saw. The subject in a very happy state of mind would sing most melodiously, not from the mouth or nose, but entirely in the breast, the sounds issuing thence." This exercise attracted the attention of all and was most heavenly. In fact, Stone and a Doctor J. P. Campbell attended to a woman exercised with singing, and they both "concluded it to be something surpassing any thing we had known in nature."[32] Clearly, then, this exercise was supernatural.

Stone admitted that some fanaticism occurred in the excitement of these revivals, but he pointed to the good effects of the exercises—especially the way they unified denominations for a moment in time. Even late in life, long after the boisterous exercises were no longer part of the movement he helped birth, Stone believed these exercises were the work of God: "After attending to many such cases," Stone wrote in the 1840s, "my conviction was complete that it was a good work—the work of God; nor has my mind wavered since on the side. . . . When I am always hurt to hear people speak lightly of this work. I always think they speak of what they know nothing about."[33] As Stone put it in 1827, he and others prayed for a revival, and God "*answered by fire*; for he poured out his spirit in ways almost miraculous."[34]

Conclusion

What happened at Cane Ridge? Well, according to Stone, the fire of God happened at Cane Ridge. People fasted, prayed, sang, shared communion, camped together, preached, exhorted, shared interdenominational fellowship and tension, experienced biracial revival and racialized space (i.e., the separating of black and white people), and—most memorably—many people participated in religious exercises and experienced the grace of God in new birth conversion.

But when summed up like that, it seems too tidy, too tame. So allow me to conclude by giving an answer to our question about what happened at Cane Ridge from the perspective of an 1819 account:

> At night, the whole scene was awfully sublime. The ranges of tents, the fires, reflecting light amidst the branches of the towering trees; the candles and lamps illuminating the encampment; hundreds moving to and fro, with lights or torches, like Gideon's army; the preaching, praying, singing and shouting all heard at once, rushing from different parts of the ground, like the sound of many waters, was enough to swallow up all the powers of contemplation. Sinners falling, and shrieks and cries for mercy awakened in the mind . . . that scene, when the awful sound will be heard, "arise ye dead and come to Judgment!"[35]

NOTES

[1]Conkin, *Cane Ridge*, ix.

[2]Conkin, *Cane Ridge*, 68.

[3]Conkin, *Cane Ridge*, 89.

[4]Stone, *Biography*, 37.

[5]Woodward, "Letter from a Brother to His Sister," 57. For the full letter, see the Appendix.

[6]Conkin, *Cane Ridge*, 84–87.

[7]Gorman, *Among the Early Evangelicals*, 25–94.

[8]Conkin, *Cane Ridge*, 59.

[9]Conkin, *Cane Ridge*, 73.

[10]Woodward, *Surprising Accounts*, 57; Conkin, *Cane Ridge*, 91, 154, 170–77.

[11]This section relies on my chapter, Gorman, "Evangelical Revivalism and Race Relations," 21–38; quotes from Conkin, *Cane Ridge*, 118; Stone, *Biography*, 44.

[12]M'Gready, "Sermon XXI: The Qualifications and Duties of a Minister," 1:314.

[13]Woodward, *Surprising Accounts*, 57; Conkin, *Cane Ridge*, 85.

[14]Stone, *Biography*, 37.

[15]Boles, *The Great Revival*, 111–21.

[16]Conkin, *Cane Ridge*, 91.

[17]Boles, *The Great Revival*, 31–35.

[18]Boles, *The Great Revival*, 121.

[19]Boles, *The Great Revival*, 121–24; Bruce, "Camp Meetings," 1:347–52.

[20]Stone, "History of the Christian Church. No. I," 76.

[21]See chapter 6 in Stone, *Biography*, 39–42.

[22]Conkin finds estimates of 300 to 1,000 more likely. McNemar, *The Kentucky Revival*, 25; Conkin, *Cane Ridge*, 92; Armenius, "Account of the Rise and Progress," 272.

[23]Stone, *Biography*, 39.

[24]McNemar, *The Kentucky Revival*, 24.

[25]Latrobe, "Plan of the Camp, August 8, 1809."

[26]Stone, *Biography*, 40. See the excerpt in the Appendix.

[27]Stone, *Biography*, 40.

[28]Stone, *Biography*, 40.

[29]Stone, *Biography*, 41.

[30]Stone, *Biography*, 41.

[31]Stone, *Biography*, 41.

[32]Stone, *Biography*, 41–42.

[33]Stone, *Biography*, 35.

[34]Stone, "History of the Christian Church. No. I," 74.

[35]Armenius, "Account of the Rise and Progress," 273.

PART II

EXPLORING CANE RIDGE

CHAPTER FOUR

Cane Ridge as a Communion Festival

JOHN MARK HICKS

Cane Ridge, though arguably the birth of camp meetings on the American frontier, was not conceived as a camp meeting but as a communion or sacramental festival.

Camp meetings peppered the landscape of nineteenth-century America, not just on the frontier but also in places like New York and New England. They began on the frontier where people lodged in portable facilities, such as wagons and tents, and listened to preaching over several days. Over time, camps became cabins, and the camp meeting evolved into annual or semi-annual events at established locations. They became a primary vehicle for revival throughout the nineteenth century. They also developed into second-blessing (sanctification) revivals, in addition to evangelistic revivals within the Holiness movement. Ultimately, in fact, camp meetings became primarily Methodist, Holiness, and eventually Pentecostal events.

In the past, many identified Cane Ridge as a camp meeting. For example, William Garrett West's important 1954 biography of Barton W. Stone regularly referred to the gatherings of the Great Revival in Kentucky as camp meetings, including Cane Ridge.[1] Many families did camp at Cane Ridge, and some estimated as many as 140 or more wagons were there in addition to other wheeled carriages. G. Baxter, who was present at Cane Ridge as well as at several other revival meetings that year, noted that "the practice of camping on the ground was introduced" at Cane Ridge.[2] Stone himself believed "this was the beginning and introduction of camp meetings."[3] The Methodist Peter Cartwright, who was also present at Cane Ridge, described it as "the first camp-meeting ever held in the United States, and here our camp-meetings took their rise."[4] The sheer size of the numbers at Cane Ridge popularized a camp meeting style that stoked the fires of revival among nineteenth-century evangelicals, especially among Methodists and later in the Holiness movement.

The Presbyterian Communion Festival

Cane Ridge, however, was, in fact, a communion festival.[5] It was a sacramental event whose climactic moment was Sunday communion at tables. Unlike camp meetings, these annual events were located at established ecclesial communities such as the Cane Ridge congregation, and they were only practiced by Presbyterian churches whose lineage was Scottish or Scots-Irish.

Typically, a communion festival was conducted in the following way. As potential communicants arrived, they prepared themselves with fasting. Thursday was typically a fast day. On Friday evening, they listened to preaching and spent the evening in prayer. Saturday was designed as a day of preparation where they continued to listen to preaching, received exhortations, engaged in prayer, and were examined by ordained ministers as to their readiness for communion. The examination involved a series of questions, but the most important question was typically something like: "Can you explain how you have experienced a quickening from the dead through Christ and in your Christian life?" or "Would you give a testimony as to how you were made alive spiritually or how Christ is precious to you?" These testimonies were often deeply emotional. If, in the judgment of the ordained ministers (or session), they were sufficiently prepared, they received a token which would admit them to the table the next day.

On Sunday, the church building was arranged with long tables (typically in the shape of a cross), and the communicants would sit at the tables after turning in their tokens. They received large portions of bread and wine, similar to what they would consume at a typical meal. The event was deeply reverential but emotional, and it was not uncommon for deep emotions to emerge in the context of the table. The communicants would come in groups of fifty to a hundred and rotate through the event until everyone who had a token participated. Monday was the day of thanksgiving. The communicants gathered for final sermons, prayers, and thanksgivings for the weekend event. The meeting typically disbanded on Monday, and people returned to their homes. Cane Ridge was atypical in that people stayed through Wednesday, perhaps into Thursday as well.

When the Cane Ridge church hosted a communion festival, it was neither unique nor innovative. It was one of eleven communion festivals that summer in Kentucky held by Presbyterians. This continued a practice that had begun among Scottish Presbyterians perhaps as early as 1590 and was commonly practiced in Scotland by the 1620s. Leigh Eric Schmidt considers Cane Ridge "not as an

American birthplace, but as a culminating event in a transatlantic exchange of religious practices."[6]

At the same time, communion festivals often exploded with revival accompanied by physical manifestations of the Holy Spirit. The most famous example of this was the "Cambuslang Work" held in August 1742, where almost 30,000 people gathered to hear George Whitefield preach in Cambuslang, Scotland. Ultimately 3,000 communed at tables on August 15, and the "holy fair" participated in a revival that consumed most of 1742 in that part of Scotland. Manifestations of the Holy Spirit included fainting spells, violent and painful contortions, and long nights of wailing as people sought God's grace.[7] What happened at Cane Ridge was not unusual but shared in a long tradition of both Holy Spirit revival and table communion. What Cambuslang symbolized for the First Great Awakening in the British Isles, Cane Ridge symbolized for the Second Great Awakening in the United States.

Communion Festival at Cane Ridge

Whatever the numbers were at Cane Ridge—estimates ranged from 10,000 to 30,000—"the majority of people at Cane Ridge," according to Paul Conkin, "were casual visitors or outsiders, some only curious spectators." Ultimately, only 800 to 1,100 actually qualified for and participated in the communion service.[8] But that is no small number when the population of Kentucky was only 220,000. In other words, perhaps 10 percent of Kentucky's population attended Cane Ridge in one way or another, and 1 percent of the population communed together at the same table in the Cane Ridge meetinghouse.

The communion table, however, was a hindrance to unity, and ultimately it was a hindrance to revival as well. Shortly after Cane Ridge, the camp meeting movement generally ditched the communion festival (though it continued in many places), and especially as Methodists and Baptists took the lead in camp meeting practices, the sacrament was dropped. Typically, Presbyterians did not admit Methodists to their table, and Baptists did not admit Presbyterians to their table. The table was fenced; it was *closed* communion. And this did not foster unity. Whatever expression of unity revivalism entailed, that unity could not find full expression at the table. Baptists and Methodists were present at Cane Ridge, and they preached on stumps and under tents. But they were "not invited to preach in Stone's meetinghouse." Presbyterian clergy examined potential communicants, but, according to Richard Shiels, "no one else was invited to commune."[9]

However, Stone, according to Newell Williams, wanted a "united sacrament" at Cane Ridge.[10] And this may have been the case, though details are murky. According to a letter from an unnamed gentleman to his sister in Philadelphia, Pennsylvania, written in August 1801, the Presbyterians and Methodists were in "full communion" on this day and even Baptists were given communion tokens if they applied for them.[11] It appears that Baptists and Methodists were given access to the table though "only Presbyterian ministers presided."[12] This is even more notable when we remember that there were only 1,741 official members of the Methodist Church in Kentucky, and the Baptists—more than likely—only exceeded the Presbyterian number of 2,000 active members by very little. In other words, there were only about 6,000 practicing Christians from these three groups in Kentucky. More than 15 percent of this number communed together at the table of the Lord.[13]

An open table became Stone's practice, inviting Christians to tear down the fences around the table. He regularly promoted the view that revivals and open tables go together. For example, Stone published a report from Thomas Allen about a four-day meeting in Harrodsburg, Kentucky. Allen wrote:

> A great number surrounded the table of the Lord; among the number were many Methodists, whose hearts seemed warmed by the love of God; and some of the Presbyterians, members of Mr. Cleland's congregation, could not be restrained from uniting with God's people in commemorating the dying sufferings of our common Lord. They participated with us in every part of our worship, with much satisfaction throughout the meeting.[14]

After quoting this same letter, Jason Fikes notes that Allen's report was "typical, and Stone included letters like these that alluded to communion as a happy scene where Methodists and Baptists surrounded the table together."[15]

Fikes's article tracks Stone's movement from annual sacramental festivals to weekly Lord's Supper, and at every point along the way, Stone assumes, rejoices over, and argues for a common table inclusive of Presbyterians, Methodists, Baptists, and his own Christian movement. In particular, as Fikes observes, Stone refused to exclude people who confessed Jesus as Lord and "honestly sought to obey him."[16] Moreover, Stone also refused to make the frequency of communion a test of fellowship even though he ultimately preferred weekly communion.[17] In fact, he came to see it as part of the restoration of the church itself. "Whenever the church shall be restored to her former glory," he wrote, "she will again receive the Lord's supper on every first day of the week. Certainly, then, Christians should seriously take this subject into consideration and reform."[18]

The Stone-Campbell Movement and Table Communion

When we recognize the origins of Cane Ridge in the sacramental festivals of Scots-Irish Presbyterians, we see the overlapping connection between what moved Stone and what moved Thomas and Alexander Campbell toward a more compelling vision of unity.

On the western frontier of Pennsylvania, Thomas Campbell was defrocked in 1808, in part, for welcoming people to the table from outside the narrow parameters of his Presbyterian denomination. In Glasgow, Scotland, Alexander Campbell refused to participate in a communion service that involved the use of tokens and assumed denominational loyalty. Though geographically separated, father and son together moved toward a vision of the communion table as the embodiment and display of Christian unity.

In the 1844 *Millennial Harbinger* Thomas Campbell, at the age of eighty-one, published "An Address to All Our Christian Brethren" in which he defined "Christian brethren" the same way he did in his 1809 *Declaration and Address*: "All that love our Lord Jesus Christ, in sincerity, throughout the churches."[19] He called Christians to love each other and rooted this in "the grand fundamental lesson of the gospel," which is that God so loved the world that God gave the Son so that everyone who believes might experience salvation.[20] This "grand fundamental lesson" is affirmed and experienced, he believed, in

> the three grand comprehensive positive, ordinances of the gospel; namely, baptism, the Lord's supper, and the Lord's day, all designed to keep the blissful subject of our present and eternal salvation, in its causes, effects, and consequences, before our minds: and one day every week publicly set apart for those joyful purposes.[21]

For Barton W. Stone, Thomas Campbell, and Alexander Campbell the table of the Lord was the communal moment that displayed the unity of the body of Christ. The table is a tangible, concrete manifestation of the unity of the believers who confess

Jesus is Lord. Though it was not an absolute requirement for a true and faithful church for any of these forefathers, weekly communion was a spiritual habit that formed believers into the image of Christ and assured them of their forgiveness. Through the table, they concretely and visibly participated in the unity of the Spirit.

Ultimately, the Restoration movement settled into the practice of neither inviting nor debarring anyone from the table. Participation in the table was left to the individual. Stone himself was one of the first, it appears, to suggest this practice in the swirling debate over open or closed communion.[22] At the same time, the communal nature of the table invites all who confess Jesus as Lord to sit at the Lord's table and thereby exhibit their common union (or communion). To exclude people from the table who confess Jesus as Lord or to fail to invite them is a concession to the kingdom of darkness and subverts the visible unity of the body of Christ.

The practice of the Lord's supper at Cane Ridge, where Presbyterians, Methodists, and Baptists communed at the same table, invites imitation. A unity movement cannot fence the table and issue tokens. Rather, it invites all believers to the table and shares the body and blood of Christ as the one body of Christ, the church.

NOTES

[1]West, *Barton Warren Stone*, 19–46.

[2]Woodward, "Letter from a Brother to His Sister." For the full letter, see the Appendix.

[3]Stone, "History of the Christian Church, No. I," 76.

[4]Cartwright, *Autobiography*, 34. See the Appendix.

[5]Leigh Eric Schmidt has made this case convincingly. See Schmidt, *Holy Fairs*. See also Conkin, *Cane Ridge*, 64–114.

[6]Schmidt, "'A Practical Remembrance,'" 39.

[7] Fawcett, *The Cambuslang Revival.*
[8] Conkin, *Cane Ridge*, 89, 92.
[9] Shiels, "America's Pentecost," 92.
[10] Williams, *Barton Stone: A Spiritual Biography*, 60.
[11] Woodward, *Surprising Accounts*, 58.
[12] Conkin, *Cane Ridge*, 90.
[13] Conkin, *Cane Ridge*, 81.
[14] Allen, "Letters on Revivals," 190.
[15] Fikes, "From Sacramental Season," 76.
[16] Fikes, "From Sacramental Season," 78.
[17] Stone, "The Conference in Terra Confusa," 152–53.
[18] Stone, "Query," 229. Cited by Fikes, "From Sacramental Season," 79.
[19] Thomas Campbell, "An Address," 199.
[20] Campbell, "An Address," 201.
[21] Campbell, "An Address," 202.
[22] Fikes, "From the Sacramental Season," 78, makes this claim, citing Stone, "Stone's Reply to Doctor Stephen Roach's Letter," 62–63.

CHAPTER FIVE

Barton Stone, Cane Ridge, and Slavery

RICHARD T. HUGHES

The first thing to be said about Barton Stone is that he refused to read the biblical text through the lens of American culture. Instead, he read American culture through the lens of the biblical text. That is why Stone was convinced that the ultimate test of a transformed life was not the jerks nor the barks but a life of radical discipleship. And the idea of "gospel-liberty" meant far more to Stone than freedom to claim salvation. It also meant freedom to follow the radical Jesus who stood with the poor, the marginalized, the dispossessed, and those whose race or gender made them objects of scorn and rejection.

This essay draws heavily from two of my other essays "'The Politics of the Day,' and 'The Politics of Heaven,'" 15-35.

Indeed, a countercultural principle, rooted in the biblical text, lived in the heart of Stone at least from 1797 when he was twenty-five years old. Four years later, in 1801, the Cane Ridge revival fanned that principle into a white-hot passion that drove Stone's commitment for the rest of his life.

I once described that countercultural principle as Stone's apocalyptic worldview that "led Stone and many of his followers to act as though the final rule of the kingdom of God were present in the here and now." Indeed, Stone and his people "lived their lives in the shadow of the second coming and thought of themselves as pilgrims who affirmed their allegiance to the kingdom of God rather than to the popular values of the world."[1]

The South Carolina Experience

The year 1797 was pivotal for Barton Stone, for in that year he visited Wadmalaw Island and Johns Island in South Carolina, where he witnessed white "Christian" slaveholders living in opulence while they terrorized the people they had enslaved. Stone reflected on that scene in his autobiography:

> [I] received the most friendly attention [there] of gentlemen professing religion, living in splendid palaces, surrounded with a rich profusion of luxuries, and of every thing desirable. . . . But in the midst of all this glory, my soul sickened at the sight of slavery in more horrid forms than I had ever seen it before; poor negroes! Some chained to their work—some wearing iron collars—all half naked, and followed and driven by the merciless lash of a gentleman overseer—distress appeared scowling in every face.

Then Stone made the telling statement: "This was the exciting cause of my abandonment of slavery."[2]

In addition to his graphic description of the terrors of American slavery, several phrases in this report are especially significant. The first is his statement, "This was the exciting cause of my abandonment of slavery." It is important to note that in turning his back on slavery, Stone turned his back on the laws of the United States, rejected popular values, and began his embrace of an apocalyptic worldview.

The only way to ignore the apocalyptic dimensions of Stone's theology in 1797 is to ignore—or fail to recognize—two competing realities: (1) Stone's utter commitment to God's rule in his life, already well in place by 1797, and (2) the utter brutality of slavery. What Stone witnessed on those islands forced him to choose between the rule of God, on the one hand, and the laws of the United States that sustained American slavery, on the other. He clearly chose the kingdom of God, a decision that reflected his already well-developed apocalyptic perspective.

Indeed, in a letter Stone wrote around 1800 to Samuel Rennels, pastor of the Paris, Kentucky, Presbyterian Church, Stone said of slavery, "Christians ought not to let civil policy oppose the express will of God. If we know God's will, we are not to enquire whether it will be [in] our interest to do it."[3]

The second significant phrase in Stone's report is his description of the "gentlemen *professing religion*" (italics mine). When Stone contrasted those "gentlemen" who lived "in splendid palaces, surrounded with a rich profusion of luxuries"—when he contrasted that reality with the terror those very same gentlemen inflicted on the enslaved people, Stone could only conclude that these "gentlemen" were hardly serious Christians, a point he underscored when he used the word "professing."

Stone's comment about the "gentlemen professing religion" leveled a scathing indictment, to be sure. But it was hardly as scathing as some of the comments offered by the black abolitionist,

Frederick Douglass, in a speech he delivered in 1852, eight years after Stone had died. At the very least, Douglass helps us understand the realities of American slavery that made such an impression on Stone in 1797. And he helps us understand those "gentlemen professing religion" and the depravity of significant segments of the American church. Douglass called his speech "What to the Slave is the Fourth of July?"

> The church of this country is not only indifferent to the wrongs of the slave, it actually takes sides with the oppressors. . . . It is . . . a religion which favors the rich against the poor; which exalts the proud above the humble; which divides mankind into two classes, tyrants and slaves; which says to the man in chains, *stay there*, and to the oppressor, *oppress on*; it is a religion which may be professed and enjoyed by all the robbers and enslavers of mankind; it makes God a respecter of persons, denies his fatherhood of the race, and tramples in the dust the great truth of the brotherhood of man. All this we affirm to be true of the popular church, and the popular worship of our land and nation—a religion, a church, and a worship which, on the authority of inspired wisdom, we pronounce to be an abomination in the sight of God.[4]

It is therefore little wonder that Stone viewed much of what passed for Christianity in the United States as little more than a sham, especially when compared with the standard of the kingdom of God whose citizens, according to Scripture, fed the hungry, clothed the naked, and gave the thirsty something to drink (Matthew 25). That commitment helps explain, at least in part, why Stone resigned his ministry in two Presbyterian congregations in

1803 in order "that my labors should henceforth be directed to advance the Redeemer's kingdom, irrespective of party."

Traditionally, historians have used Stone's phrase, "irrespective of party," to argue that his rejection of sectarianism was the driving force behind his departure from the Presbyterian ministry. And while that is true, his commitment to the kingdom of God was a driving force as well, even though that commitment meant a life of poverty. In truth, Stone connected his rejection of sectarianism with his rejection of slavery.

> Thus to the cause of truth I sacrificed the friendship of two large congregations, and an abundant salary for the support of myself and family. . . . I preferred honesty and a good conscience to all these things. Having now no support from the congregations, and having emancipated my slaves, I turned my attention cheerfully, though awkwardly, to labor on my little farm. . . . I relaxed not in my ministerial labors, preaching almost every night, and often in the day time [as well]. . . . I had no money to hire laborers, and often on my return home, I found the weeds were getting ahead of my corn. I had often to labor at night while others were asleep, to redeem my lost time.[5]

The Cane Ridge Revival, the Holy Spirit, and the Rejection of Slavery

While the inter-denominational cooperation that marked the Cane Ridge Revival encouraged Stone to reject sectarianism, the outpouring of the Holy Spirit that he and thousands of others experienced there strengthened his resolve against the institution of slavery.

Just a few weeks before the outbreak of the Cane Ridge Revival,[6] Stone married Elizabeth Campbell, who owned two slaves, a man and a woman. In his old age, Stone recalled that shortly after the close of the revival, his "mind became unearthly, and was solely engaged in the work of the Lord. I had emancipated my slaves from a sense of right, choosing poverty with a good conscience, in preference to all the treasures of the world." Indeed, he wrote, "This revival cut the bonds of many poor slaves."

Stone clearly believed that a cold, formalized religion "of decency and order," like the religion practiced by so many opponents of the great revival, had no power to convict slave-holding Christians that slavery was a heinous sin. At the same time, he believed that the Holy Spirit, so much at work in the Great Revival, was the singular force that prompted many to free their slaves. In his judgment, the fact that so many veterans of the Cane Ridge Revival had freed their slaves "speaks volumes in favor of the work. For of what avail," he asked, "is a religion of decency and order, without righteousness?"

Further evidence that the Spirit-filled Great Revival prompted many to free their slaves comes from Newell Williams, who reports that "the Presbyterian ministers who supported the revival were, like Stone, staunch emancipationists."[7] According to Williams, the records of Bourbon County where the Cane Ridge Revival took place reveal that members of the Cane Ridge Church filed twenty-nine deeds of manumission between 1801 and 1819.[8]

The centrality of the commitment of Stone and his followers to enslaved people is reflected in the autobiography of Joseph Thomas, a North Carolinian who visited the Stoneite communities in Kentucky in 1810/11:

> The Christian companies in this settlement and about Cane Ridge have been large; but within a few years,

> many of them, who held black people as slaves, emancipated them, and have moved to the state of Ohio. I will observe that the Christians of these parts *abhor* the idea of *slavery*, and some of them have almost tho't that they who hold to slavery cannot be a Christian.[9]

An Older Barton Stone, the Kingdom of God, and the Anti-Slavery Impulse

By 1835, Stone's passion to abolish slavery led him to reprint in his *Christian Messenger* a statement on slavery by a man considered radical in both the North and the South. That man was William Lloyd Garrison, whose statement "Address to the People of the United States on Slavery" called for the *immediate* abolition of slavery, something to which Stone could assent but with which most southern whites, including most southern white Christians, would never agree. And because of threats of violence against abolitionists, presumably including himself, he discontinued publication of Garrison's "Address" after only three installments.

It is worth noting, however, that Stone prefaced the first installment of Garrison's "Address" with a statement of his own conviction: "I have long viewed Slavery as the darkest cloud that hangs over America."[10] Indeed, he had—ever since 1797, when he witnessed the terror inflicted on enslaved people by those "gentlemen professing religion" but "living in splendid palaces."

By 1842, as Williams notes, Stone had lost faith in the American government and, with that turn of mind, his apocalyptic orientation reached new heights. No longer did he simply seek to live his life *as if* God's sovereignty over all the earth and the rule of the kingdom of God were fully present in his own time and place. Now he pledged his exclusive allegiance to the kingdom of

God and withdrew his allegiance from the government of the United States.

As Williams shows, he lost faith in the American government, first, because politics in the United States had taken on such highly partisan dimensions. But he also lost faith because of the failure of the American government to banish slavery.[11] Accordingly, in an 1843 essay that Stone appropriately titled "Reflections of Old Age," he asked these probing questions:

> Must we conclude . . . that our Congress and State legislatures, are schools of corruption and demoralization?—that the departments of state are nurseries of vice and irreligion?—and that the politics of the day are in opposition to the politics of heaven?—Dreadful conclusion! Yet how can we evade it . . . ?[12]

A year later, in 1844, Stone composed a fictitious conversation between an old preacher and a young preacher and has the old man say:

> We must return to the government, laws and ordinances of our rightful king, the Lord Jesus, before we shall be ever gathered together and become worthy subjects of his kingdom. We must unite our energies, advance the government and kingdom of our Lord, and meddle not with the government of this world, whether human, ecclesiastical, or political, or civil; all others aside from that of heaven will be put down by a firm decree of our Lord before the end come.

To that radical statement, the young preacher protested, invoking Romans 13:1—"Let every person be subject to the governing authorities." "You astonish me," the young preacher said. "Are not the civil powers and governments that be, ordained of God?

And is it not the duty of Christians to be subject to them, and to sustain them?"

To that question, the old preacher—clearly, Barton W. Stone himself—had given much thought.

> If it be the duty of Christians under one worldly government to uphold and support that government, then it is the duty of Christians living in every worldly government to uphold and support that government; those living in N. America must uphold and support the [slaveholding] democracy of the United States; those in Britain, must support the monarchy of England; those in Russia, must support the despotism there; those at Rome, most [*sic*] support the government of the pope, the man of sin, the antichrist of our rightful Lord;—those in South America must support every petty tyrant that wades through blood to sit in the supreme chair of state. . . . Can we for one moment think that the Lord enjoined on his people under the Cesars [*sic*] of old to uphold and defend their bloody governments, which enjoined the extirpation of the Christians, or to force them to abandon their religions and sacrifice to idols?[13]

Stone's conclusion came in the form of two rhetorical questions, and then a resounding answer. "Must we be subject to all these powers, never resist them, but always obey them? Did the Apostles resist the higher powers when they were forbidden to teach in the name of Jesus? Nay—they chose to obey God rather than man."[14]

By embracing that conclusion, Stone tapped into that great counternarrative in the biblical text that summons Christians to resist imperial powers that seek to usurp the throne of God. And he took his place in that community of American theologians who, throughout the history of the American nation, have grasped the truth that "the biblical topic is politics," who have read American culture through the lens of the biblical text, and who have understood—and still understand—that the drama played out in that text is the struggle between the kingdoms of earth and *the* kingdom of God.

NOTES

[1] I have borrowed the pregnant and highly descriptive phrase "in the shadow of the second coming" from Weber, *Living in the Shadow of the Second Coming*. See also Hughes, *Reviving the Ancient Faith*, 92–93.

[2] Stone, *Biography*, 27–28.

[3] "B. W. Stone to Samuel Rennels," Cane Ridge Preservation Project Museum, Cane Ridge, Kentucky, n.d., cited in Williams, "Pursuit of Justice," 5. This essay is an excellent account of Stone's antislavery attitudes and activities.

[4] Douglass, "What, to the Slave, Is the Fourth of July?" 262–63.

[5] Stone, *Biography*, 50.

[6] Stone, *Biography*, 37.

[7] Williams, "Pursuit of Justice," 6; see also Williams, *Barton Stone: A Spiritual Biography*, 65–78.

[8] Williams, "Pursuit of Justice," 6–7 and especially n. 14.

[9] Thomas, *The Travels and Gospel Labors*, 56.

[10] Stone, comments preceding Garrison, "Address to the People," 82.

[11] Williams, "From Trusting Congress," 73.

[12] Stone, "Reflections of Old Age," 123.

[13] Stone, "An Interview between an Old and Young Preacher," 227–28.

[14] Stone, "Reply to T. P. Ware," 169–70.

CHAPTER SIX

"The Reproof of a Weak Woman"

Women Exhorters at Cane Ridge

JAMES L. GORMAN

Barton Stone visited the Logan County revivals during the spring of 1801, when he saw many experience the falling exercise. People lay sometimes for hours in a motionless state until they obtained deliverance. And then they exhorted those around them in the crowd:

> They would rise shouting deliverance, and then would address the surrounding multitude in language truly eloquent and impressive. With astonishment did I hear men, women, and children declaring the wonderful works of God, and the glorious mysteries of the gospel. Their appeals were solemn, heart-penetrating, bold and free. Under such addresses many others would fall down into the same state from which the speakers had just been delivered.[1]

Descriptions like this one in Stone's autobiography appear in many of the sources that document Cane Ridge and the Great Revival in the West—letters, diaries, sermons, and autobiographies. They depict women, black people, and children exhorting those around them, often awakening others to their sinfulness and leading them into new birth conversion.

Even an avid reader of American religious history will more than likely not have read about the countless women who exhorted and sometimes even preached during the one hundred years between 1740 and 1840. And that is because most American historians until recent decades have neglected the stories of these evangelical women preachers and exhorters. This chapter explores examples of female exhortation at Cane Ridge and, more broadly, in evangelical revivalism during the early national era before offering several explanations for the acceptance of female exhortation at the time.

Women's Public Speech

Thankfully, in 1998, historian Catherine Brekus wrote a groundbreaking book that provides an authoritative guide to the rich and complex history of female preaching and exhorting.[2] Brekus identifies three distinct types of women's public speech that took place during the Great Revival in the West—praying, testifying or witnessing, and exhorting. Praying aloud was the most common and least controversial act of speaking. Women invoked God to change hearts, to forgive sins, to show compassion, to provide strength, and send new birth to all those in need of conversion. Testifying or witnessing included declaration of God's mighty acts or, as Stone put it, "declaring the wonderful works of God, and the glorious mysteries of the gospel." Exhortation utilized prayer and testifying, but it typically referred more specifically to words of warning. Exhorters admonished sinners around them to seek salvation, and they guided people through the conversion experience. Sometimes, exhorters would cite biblical passages, so the line between exhortation and preaching often blurred, especially in the chaos of a camp meeting revival.[3]

Evangelicals distinguished between exhorting and preaching. Preaching was planned and formal exposition of scripture; exhorting was spontaneous and informal. Preaching took place in the pulpit or preaching stand; exhorting took place in the pew or field. "Preachers were authoritative *teachers* who were experts on God's sacred word."[4] Again, these careful distinctions did not always hold in the heat of a revival.

Most of the southern revivalists associated with Cane Ridge did not permit women to preach, but they did encourage female exhortation, even though they debated what exhortation entailed. For example, in his 1803 sermon on the revival in Kentucky, leading revivalist David Rice supported lay exhortation, but his narrow definition especially regarding female exhortation revealed his anxiety about the revival's challenge to traditional gender and religious hierarchies. Rice argued that the traditional Presbyterian practice of opposing lay exhorting was wrong because it precluded the spread of the gospel. If a man or a woman exhorted people around them, it might have even more effect than a discourse from the pulpit. However, if exhortation by either men or women was done "with an air of domination or authority, as if by a commission from heaven, and stern commanding countenance," then the practice was unacceptable. Rice continued, "No impulse, however strong, . . . can justify a woman in laying aside her proper, native modesty and delicacy, and assuming a masculine boldness, or a liberty unbecoming her sex. . . . A woman by deviating a little from female modesty may do more injury to the cause of Christ and to precious souls, than ever she will do by all her most pathetic exhortations."[5] Rice reflected the common understanding of femininity as modest, delicate, and constrained, and any type of exhortation that compromised a woman's femininity necessarily compromised the gospel.

On the other end of the spectrum was Richard McNemar, the Presbyterian leader who penned the "Last Will and Testament of the Springfield Presbytery" and eventually became a Shaker. Throughout his 1807 pamphlet on the Kentucky Revival, McNemar viewed exhortation in the revivals as an apostolic gift given to people of all ages, races, and sexes as a clear sign of at least two things: (1) God authored the revivals and (2) the imminent last days.[6] For example, McNemar wrote about the Kentucky revivals in 1801:

> To see a bold Kentuckian (undaunted by the horrors of war) turn pale and tremble at the reproof of a weak woman, a little boy, or a mean African; to see him sink down in deep remorse, roll and toss, and gnash his teeth, till black in the face; intreat the prayers of those he came to devour, and through their fervent intercessions and kind instructions, obtain deliverance, and return in the possession of the meek and gentle spirit which he set out to oppose—who would say the change was not supernatural and miraculous?[7]

McNemar's comments reveal the typical white male understanding at the time—women were the weaker sex and Africans were small-minded and of little consequence. For McNemar, the exhortations of women that brought the "bold" male warrior into the conversion experience and made him meek and gentle in spirit could only be interpreted as a miracle. Not only the presence of women exhorters but the efficacy of their exhortations to convert hard sinners was proof of God's work in the revivals.

Female Exemplars

Among the revivalists, whether a conservative David Rice or a radical Richard McNemar, female exhortation was expected and encouraged. In fact, female examples occurred more often than male examples in the accounts I examined. Further, according to one account by James McGready, the 1797 revival in Logan County, which could be considered the beginning of the Second Great Awakening, began with a female exhorter. A woman, whose name McGready did not provide, who had long been a member of the Presbyterian Church was struck with deep conviction. After a few days, she was filled with joy in her belief and immediately visited friends and relatives "from house to house, and warned them of their danger in a most solemn, faithful manner, and plead with them to repent and seek religion. This, as a means, was accompanied with the divine blessing to the awakening of many."[8] In other words, when this woman exhorted, people converted and revivals began.

In his description of the falling exercise, Stone singled out the experience of two young sisters to illustrate the conversion process, providing clues about the content of lay exhortation. The two sisters both fell when they were attending to the exercises and the preaching at the time. Both lay for more than an hour in a lifeless state. Then they showed signs of life, crying for mercy but looking very gloomy. Finally, the gloom turned to heavenly smiles. One of them cried out praising Jesus and then "spoke of the love of God—the preciousness of Jesus, and of the glory of the gospel, to the surrounding crowd, in language almost superhuman, and pathetically exhorted all to repentance." The other sister did the same a little while after. Stone said he had seen many pious people follow this process, ending with exhortation, "speaking like angels to all around."[9]

But most impressive to eyewitnesses were exhortations from young girls, and one striking anecdote comes from the Cane Ridge revival. At about seven years old, Barbara made an impression on many around her. She was on a man's shoulders so she could speak to the multitude. She exhorted until she appeared exhausted and rested her head on the man carrying her. Someone in the crowd said, "Poor thing, she had better be laid down," "at which she quickly turned round her head, and said, 'Don't call me poor, for Christ is my brother, God my father, and I have a kingdom to inherit, therefore don't call me poor, for I am rich in the blood of the Lamb.'"[10]

McGready recorded an anecdote providing content from an exhortation of another "little girl":

> I stood by her whilst she lay across her mother's lap almost in despair. I was conversing with her when the first gleam of light broke in upon her mind—She started to her feet, and in an ecstacy of joy, she cried out, "O he is willing, he is willing—he is come, he is come—O what a sweet Christ he is—O what a precious Christ he is—O what a fulness I see in him—O what a beauty I see in him—O why was it that I never could believe! that I never could come to Christ before, when Christ was so willing to save me?" Then turning round, she addressed sinners, and told them of the glory, willingness and preciousness of Christ, and plead with them to repent; and all this in language so heavenly, and, at the same time, so rational and scriptural, that I was filled with astonishment. But were I to write you every particular of this kind that I have been an eye and ear witness to, during the two past years, it would fill many sheets of paper.[11]

In the case of Stone, two little girls were the first to experience exercises after he returned from the Logan County revivals in 1801. The night of his return, when he preached at his Concord congregation, "two little girls were struck down under the preaching of the word, and in every respect were exercised as those were in the south of Kentucky, as already described." Then without any commentary, he said, the little girls' "addresses made deep impressions on the congregations."[12]

The egalitarian effects of new birth theology and democratic revivalism created space not only for white women and children exhorters but also for black female exhorters. Although I do not have any accounts of black female exhorters at Cane Ridge (almost certainly some black women would have exhorted there), in a letter written in January 1802, James McCorkle gave an account of a biracial revival in Randolph, North Carolina, where a two-thousand-member gathering underwent a sudden burst of ecstatic religious experiences. McCorkle wrote, "Suddenly, as if by an electric shock, a large number in every direction men, women, children, white and black, fell and cried for mercy; while others appeared, in every quarter, either praying for the fallen or exhorting bye-standers to repent and believe." Making his way through the crowd, McCorkle was stopped by a "black-man prostrate on the ground, and his aged mother on her knees at his feet in all the agony of prayer for her son." Nearby, another "black-woman, grasping her mistress' hand, [cried] 'O mistress you prayed for me when I wanted a heart to pray for myself. Now thank God he has given me a heart to pray for you and everybody else.'"[13] This female exhorter seems to have transcended the lines of class, race, and gender in the unique context of revival.

Contextual Explanations for Female Exhortation

Why? Why was female exhortation accepted at those revivals at that time? First, historians have noted that evangelicalism had the "radical potential to suspend the distinctions of race and sex."[14] Authority to exhort rested in the individual's conversion experience rather than their race, sex, age, or clerical status. This emphasis on experiential piety gave "unprecedented authority to the laity."[15] Not only were all the converted spiritually equal before God; they were equally called to admonish the unconverted around them. In short, new birth theology provided a clear basis and justification for lay exhortation.

Second, and closely tied to new birth theology, the evangelical ritual of conversion also fostered women's public speech. Before the Great Awakening, almost no one permitted women to speak in churches, Quakers being the main exception. However, in the Great Awakening, when new birth theology and conversion rituals became the norm for evangelicals, the ritual of conversion came to include the convert crying out and testifying about God's gracious converting work. Crying out and testifying naturally came to include exhortation. For example, Richard McNemar explained that after a person obtained a hope of salvation, "under such an overpowering weight of the divine goodness . . . they were constrained to cry out, with tears and trembling, and testify a full and free salvation in Christ, for all that would come; and to warn their fellow-creatures of the danger of continuing in sin; and entreating them in the most tender and affectionate manner; to turn from it; and seek the Lord, in sure and certain hope that he would be found."[16] In other words, the very structure and flow of the conversion process carved out space for female exhortation.

Both the theology and ritual of new birth conversion in evangelical revivals contributed to the construction of religious space that transcended human and cultural boundaries—a place where God's Spirit was outpoured. To be sure, there were always David Rice figures who argued that gender norms must not be rejected in the revivals. But practically speaking, gender and racial norms were blurred as women followed the ritual process of conversion and projected their voice of exhortation to men and women near them.

Third, the outdoor context of many Second Great Awakening revivals also encouraged increased women's participation. For those who felt a call to exhort but remained intimidated in typical church settings, the open fields and wooded areas of camp meeting revivals sometimes provided just the right context for some women to lose their fears.[17]

Fourth, numerous political and social ideals encouraged lay exhortation. The early American republic raised up the individual's freedom and autonomy in society, sparking what historians call a process of democratization. Democratization encouraged a distrust of elites and hierarchies and authorities while emphasizing each individual's ability to control their own lives and government and churches. One of the signs of democratization of Christianity was lay exhorters, including women and enslaved people. Many revivalists believed an average person, including a woman or an enslaved person, had the capability of interpreting the Bible as well as a person with a divinity degree. Some female exhorters did interpret Scripture as they spoke, thereby blurring the line between exhortation and preaching.

Beyond the effects of democratization, changing conceptions of gender made female exhortation seem somewhat natural. The so-called separation of church and state or the disestablishment of religion in the 1780s took authority to govern church affairs out of the hands of the state. As a result, a competitive religious marketplace with little regulation emerged. With this kind of freedom in the religious marketplace, even firmly established gender roles could be challenged. This was the case with some women, such as Jarena Lee, whose supernatural call to preach the gospel and subsequent eloquent preaching in the 1810s encouraged Methodists to make space for female preaching.[18]

Although some women who exhorted at revivals followed paths like Lee's, most female exhorters at evangelical revivals probably simply followed the expected ritual process that included exhortation and, by doing so, contributed to a subtle change in gender norms. In fact, historian Catherine Brekus suggests that changing conceptions of femininity in the early republican context, which depicted women as naturally virtuous, gave women a new moral authority.[19] As long as women retained a posture of meekness, exhortation to those around them seemed natural.[20] Of course, patriarchy remained intact and most evangelicals embraced female exhortation but not female preaching or ordination.

Conclusion

Revivalists at Cane Ridge and elsewhere at the time typically supported female exhortation at revivals, though they understood exhortation as categorically different from preaching. Leaders at the Great Revival in the West described women of all ages and races exhorting men and women around them at revivals. Evangelicalism's theology, ritual practice, and revival space all influenced the rise and expectation of female exhortation at revivals. Furthermore, democratic impulses and the disestablishment of religion influenced both the practice of Christianity and conceptions of gender that made female exhortation seem at least acceptable, if not natural.

Of course, if one were to ask the female exhorters why they exhorted at the revivals, they would probably not point to the list I provided above. Instead, they would probably say they exhorted both to share their own experience of God's immeasurable grace and to awaken their unconverted neighbors who were in great danger of an eternity in hell.

NOTES

[1]Stone, *Biography*, 34–35.

[2]Brekus argues that, on the one hand, evangelicals forgot these women preachers because they were too radical and, on the other hand, women's rights activists found them too conservative. Most of the women preachers and exhorters during this era were evangelicals who defended female preaching but remained theologically orthodox and supported most of the gender norms of the day. Brekus, *Strangers and Pilgrims*, 7.

[3]Brekus, *Strangers and Pilgrims*, 127–32; Conkin, *Cane Ridge*, 91.

[4]Brekus, *Strangers and Pilgrims*, 132.

[5]Rice, *A Sermon on the Present Revival of Religion*, 21–22.

[6]McNemar, *The Kentucky Revival*, 33–35, 67–68.

[7]McNemar, *The Kentucky Revival*, 35.

[8]M'Gready, *Posthumous Works*, 1:ix.

[9]Stone, *Biography*, 39.

[10]Woodward, "Letter from Brother to His Sister," 58. See the Appendix.

[11]M'Gready, *Posthumous Works*, 1:xiii–xiv.

[12]Stone, *Biography*, 36.

[13]M'Corkle, "Letter from James M'Corkle Dated January 8, 1802," 21.

[14]Brekus, *Strangers and Pilgrims*, 130.

[15]Brekus, *Strangers and Pilgrims*, 36, 42.

[16]McNemar, *The Kentucky Revival*, 20.

[17]Brekus, *Strangers and Pilgrims*, 142; Bruce, "Camp Meetings," 1:350–51.

[18]Lee, *Religious Experience and Journal of Mrs. Jarena Lee*; Braude, *Sisters and Saints*, 28–31.

[19]Brekus, *Strangers and Pilgrims*, 14–15. Gender "refers to the cultural meanings that men and women have ascribed to sexual difference over time." Masculinity and femininity have changed over time, not remaining fixed. Women sometimes used their unique difference as female to justify preaching. Obviously, it was also used to suggest that their feminine characteristics barred them from the pulpit.

[20]Brekus, *Strangers and Pilgrims*, 148–49; Moore and Calhoon, "Evangelicals: Nineteenth Century," 2:800–801.

PART III

RECONSIDERING CANE RIDGE

CHAPTER SEVEN

Was Cane Ridge America's Pentecost?

LEONARD ALLEN

The title of this chapter keys off the title of Paul Conkin's excellent book *Cane Ridge: America's Pentecost* (1990). Several contemporaries of the revival were so struck by the momentous and awe-inspiring nature of this event that they could find no more apt description than this—an American Pentecost. As Conkin puts it, for the participants it was as if "the Spirit of God moved through the thickets and cane breaks with wondrous effects. The third person of the Trinity took precedence. People felt the power and received the gifts of the Holy Spirit."[1] And this empowering took place on a scale that no one present had witnessed before.

We've looked closely at the various and dramatic "exercises." Chief among them was falling, swooning, or fainting, often connected to deep groaning. And holy laughter and singing were widespread. One minister described the scene this way: "Sinners dropping down on every hand, shrieking, groaning, crying for mercy, convoluted; professors [of religion] praying, agonizing, fainting, falling down in distress, for sinners, or in raptures of joy! Some singing, some shouting, clapping their hands, hugging and even kissing. . . . No spectacle can incite a stronger sensation."[2] Visitors reported being astonished by the sheer level of noise. One minister said it was like the roar of Niagara Falls.

Though no reports indicate that anyone claimed the power of physical healing at Cane Ridge and though holy laughter, singing, and other forms of speech did not appear to be the glossolalia of later Pentecostalism, the comparison of Cane Ridge to Pentecost was not surprising. How better to capture the awesome and at times overwhelming events that unfolded there!

But to call the Cane Ridge revival a kind of Pentecost implies that it was much more than a single event marked by dramatic signs of the Spirit's presence and power. To give it the import of a Pentecost suggests that it marked and opened up something new and that its effects were long lasting and far reaching. So let's explore the impact of the revival on American Christianity and assess its legacy. In what sense can it be called America's Pentecost?

Old Lights and New Lights

First, as we have already seen, Cane Ridge was rooted in a tradition. It was not something entirely new. It was actually a communion festival following a two-hundred-year-old tradition rooted deeply in Scots-Irish Presbyterianism.[3] For serious Presbyterians these festivals were times of intense self-examination and spiritual renewal; for young people they were times of conviction and conversion (somewhat like summer camp today). Sometimes these communion festivals exploded with revival, including intense physical and emotional effects such as fainting and trance-like states.

As Scots-Irish Presbyterians immigrated to America, they brought the communion festival with them. Indeed, it was precisely this kind of sacramental service that took place at Cane Ridge in August 1801. It was the climax of a dozen or more communion festivals in central Kentucky that summer. They continued to occur into the fall of 1801, and then spread to Virginia, East Tennessee, Western Pennsylvania, the Carolinas, and Georgia the next year and beyond.[4] The ones in the Carolinas and Georgia rivaled Cane Ridge in size and intensity, though their sacramental setting steadily receded as Methodists and Baptists became a more dominant presence than Presbyterians.

In this spectacular season of revival, tension spread among Presbyterians, just as it had sixty years earlier after the great Cambuslang Revival in Scotland where George Whitfield had preached. Many clergymen, possibly a majority, had been dismayed and frightened, leading to a clear rupture in Scottish Presbyterianism—a rupture between the Old Lights and New Lights, between opponents and supporters of the revivals. The Seceder branch of the church, to which Thomas and Alexander Campbell belonged, deeply opposed such trends, viewing them as disorderly and excessive.

The same tensions exploded in the revival season in Kentucky in 1801 and the years that followed. Many Presbyterian ministers, even supporters of the revivals, were nervous about the emotionalism and the significance of the more extreme "exercises." Some foresaw disastrous consequences, ranging from the erosion of orthodoxy to the inroads of demonic forces. But some rejoiced, chief among them the host minister, Barton Stone.

As in the First Great Awakening sixty years earlier, Presbyterians agonizingly split into Old Lights and New Lights. Some of those who came to be called Old Lights or opposers of the revivals tried to articulate a balanced assessment, stressing the character of true revival: the humbled hearts of converts, the importance of preaching and prayer, confession of sin and the joy of forgiveness, the strong sense of God's presence, and moral transformation as visible fruit. At the same time they sounded warnings: too much reliance on feelings, the elevation of physical exercises (which they viewed as incidental to revival), and new and disorderly means (like the "mourner's bench"). They warned against the undermining of Calvinist orthodoxy, especially the embrace of a free-will Arminianism, which put revival too much in the realm of human initiative.

The New Light Revolt

Similarly, after 1801, the revival atmosphere precipitated a deep divide among Presbyterian ministers in Kentucky. By 1803, there was open revolt among the New Lights. Richard McNemar, a spokesman for the extreme pro-revival party who had been censured as an "Arminian" and an "enthusiast" by his presbytery, was joined by four New Light colleagues, John Thompson, Robert Marshall, John Dunleavy, and Barton Stone. They drafted a paper announcing their withdrawal from the Synod of Kentucky and claiming the authority of Scripture alone over any traditional confession of faith. They formed the Springfield Presbytery, which existed for only nine months. Then, in June 1804, during a meeting at Cane Ridge, the leaders decided to dissolve it, issuing the "Last Will and Testament of the Springfield Presbytery" (apparently written by McNemar). The Cane Ridge congregation immediately declared itself an independent Christian church with no Presbyterian ties. They adopted the simple name "Christian" and sought to dispense with all creeds but the Bible. A loose network of congregations began to form, sometimes called New Light, more often simply Christian.

The beginnings of modern-day Churches of Christ are rooted precisely here. Many years ago, R. L. Roberts argued that Churches of Christ owe their first and primary debt to Barton Stone and his "Christian" movement, not to Alexander Campbell.[5] In a groundbreaking article, Roberts traced the growth of the Stone movement from 1804 to 1832. He provided details of Stone's extensive evangelistic work, which centered in Kentucky, Ohio, and Tennessee, and chronicled the host of preachers under his influence who labored in small, mostly backwoods churches across the Ohio, Tennessee, and Mississippi valleys—men like Samuel and John Rogers, John Mulkey, Ephraim Moore, James Matthews, B. F. Hall, W. D. Jourdan, Tolbert Fanning, and Reuben Dooley.

Roberts located the strength of the Stone movement in the Cumberland Plateau region of Kentucky and Tennessee. He compiled a list of about two hundred Stoneite preachers in the Cumberland region who were establishing what they called "Churches of Christ" long before Campbell was ever known in the region. Stone himself lived just above Nashville, Tennessee, for two or three years beginning in 1812. By 1832, there were as many as 380 Stoneite churches in Tennessee and northern Alabama, most of them established by men who were largely unaware of Campbell's work. In addition, there were reports by 1824 of Stoneite preachers in Texas, and in 1835 several families—assisted by Davey Crockett—led a whole Stoneite church from West Tennessee to East Texas, from which the movement spread further west.[6]

The central themes of the movement were freedom from all creeds and restrictive human traditions, restoration of simple New Testament Christianity, the transforming power of the Holy Spirit, separation from the fashions of the world, and the coming millennial unity of believers. This unity Stone called "fire union," for he believed that any lasting unity could be forged only in the fire of God's Spirit.[7]

For the rest of his life, Barton Stone remained an ardent supporter of revival practices. Some of the physical "exercises" present in the 1801 revival, particularly the one Stone described as holy laughter or singing, apparently continued to be a part of the Cane Ridge and Concord churches for a decade or so under Stone's ministry. Further, he could continue to look with favor on the revivalist innovation called the mourner's bench. If such a practice, he said as late as 1832, was "contrary to the letter and spirit of the gospel," then "we cannot conceive how God should have blessed so many in the practice of it."[8]

America's Pentecost

So let me now return to my earlier question: In what sense can we speak of Cane Ridge as America's Pentecost? I want to give two diverging answers to this question.

First, Cane Ridge might fit that description in light of its profound effect in shaping what we can call America's evangelical pietism. Modern Christian pietism began in the early seventeenth century as a Protestant renewal movement and has since become an umbrella term for various movements that focus on the centrality of the conversion experience, on "vital piety," and on the disciplines nurturing one's interior life with God. The largest and most influential pietist movement was begun by John Wesley in the 1730s. The Wesleyan movement along with the American Calvinist Jonathan Edwards laid the foundation for a new view of conversion that emerged in the First and Second Great Awakenings in eighteenth- and nineteenth-century America. As we saw in Chapter One, we can call it new birth conversion.

This view proclaimed that God converted people by the immediate work of the Holy Spirit. And this conversion followed a basic three-part pattern: (1) an initial awakening to one's dangerous and lost spiritual condition; (2) a period of distress and deepening conviction of one's utter helplessness before God; and (3) an experience of deliverance in which the Holy Spirit filled one's heart with love for God and granted assurance of forgiveness.[9] This understanding of the Spirit and conversion became standard in the First Great Awakening in the 1740s and 50s and was developed further in the Great Revivals epitomized by Cane Ridge.

These revivals were where what came to be called American Evangelicalism was shaped. At the heart of it was a "crisis" conversion experience following the three-fold pattern: awakening, distress and conviction, and deliverance and assurance. The new evangelical pietism came to be marked by a deeply personal experience with God, an experience so powerful and central that the traditional place of the sacraments in the Christian life more and more receded. Conversion was detached from baptism, the communion table, and, indeed, from church membership. The new revival techniques became a new kind of liturgy—new modes of singing and ecstatic forms of worship, lay testimony and exhortation, special places at the front of worship spaces for sinners under conviction, and camp meetings (which soon replaced the communion festival). The trajectory of American Evangelicalism arcs, we might say, from Cane Ridge down through the revival streams that followed, including both hot forms like twentieth-century Pentecostalism and much cooler forms like Billy Graham and post-World War II Evangelicalism.

Perhaps this is justification enough for speaking of Cane Ridge as America's Pentecost.

The Campbellite Takeover

But second, Cane Ridge might fit the description as America's Pentecost in light of its effect in prompting and shaping Stone's "Christian" movement from 1804 through the late 1820s. But I qualify this with a "might" because of what happened to this movement when Alexander Campbell's theology became predominant.

Cane Ridge had a profound theological leveling effect on Stone. The theological intricacies of his creedal Presbyterianism were swept away in the powerful and transformative experiences he witnessed there. In the aura of the Spirit, a new and more direct experience of God was opened up, along with exciting new prospects for the unity of Christians. As we saw earlier, this Spirit-focused restoration movement spread throughout the Cumberland region, and in ten years or so numbered around 13,000 members.

Beginning about 1823, Campbell's message about the "ancient gospel and order of things" began to spread throughout Stone's "Christian" movement. Both movements used similar rhetoric and seemed to have strikingly similar goals. But Alexander Campbell believed that Stone's approach fell short, that his restoring work was only preliminary to true restoration. Stone had led the way in protesting against "creeds, councils, and human dogma" and urging unity upon the Bible alone. But Stone's reform movement did not provide an adequate platform for restoration and unity. Stone's work, Campbell insisted, involved "clearing the forests and burning the brush"; but he had stopped short of restoring the true faith.[10] Many new voices were arising, crying "Lo, here!" and "Lo, there!" But, Campbell insisted, "there is not one voice heard in all the world outside the boundaries of the present reformation, calling upon people to return to the *original gospel and order of things*."[11] By the mid to late 1820s Alexander believed that was precisely what he had rediscovered—nothing less than "the ancient gospel" and its essential corollary, "the ancient order of things."

The "ancient gospel," Campbell argued, was simply a series of "facts" which the New Testament placed in a particular order. New Testament preaching began with the biblical testimony to these gospel facts; this testimony, without any other supernatural agency, produced faith; and faith led a person to "obey the gospel," that is, to repent of sins and be baptized for remission of sins.

Reception of the Spirit then followed conversion.[12] Here was a new *ordo salutis* or pattern of conversion, one that utterly rejected the revivalist view.

The Stoneite "Christians" gradually adopted Campbell's anti-revivalist theology of conversion, especially after the two movements united in January 1832. Stone himself embraced it, though with some reservation and looseness. He saw its benefit to many distressed and uncertain believers, but also its downside, especially in the years following the uniting of the two movements. And as the Stoneite Christians embraced it, they underwent a profound transformation. I would argue that as the "Christian" movement converged with Campbell's Disciples (in the 1830s and beyond), the world of Cane Ridge became a forgotten and foreign world, a world mostly eclipsed by Campbell's Old Light sensibilities, his new *ordo salutis,* and his Lockean or Baconian rationalism.

A New Pattern of Conversion

Campbell was an Old Light. If Stone supported revivals, Alexander Campbell abhorred them. If Stone rejoiced in the Spirit's powerful work, Campbell was disgusted by the emotionalism in revivals. He deeply opposed what he termed "spiritual influences" in conversion. He believed that the dominant revivalist view of conversion ran roughshod over biblical teaching, opened the door to spiritual delusions, and discredited the gospel to people of reason. He could call this view of conversion "the greatest delusion of this our age, and one of the most prolific causes of the infidelity, immorality, and irreligion of our contemporaries."[13] So Campbell rejected the revivalist pattern, minimizing conversion and sanctification as "experiences" and emphasizing their rational and volitional character.

At the heart of Campbell's movement—its genius, we might say—was the message that people could bypass all the emotional paraphernalia of revivalism and use their own common sense to examine the factual testimony of Scripture, believe it, promptly "obey the gospel" (be baptized for remission of sins), and immediately receive the full assurance of salvation. The "ancient gospel," he urged, did not require a person to become "a desponding, trembling infidel before he can become a believer."[14] Conversion was a rational, quick, and simple process.

This message appealed to many people bypassed by the revival fires. Many thousands found relief for their prolonged but unresolved Calvinistic distress in this simple, rational path to salvation.[15] It was this message, more than anything else, that launched and propelled Campbell's new movement. And with the union of the two movements in January 1832, it was this message, and the theology that undergirded it, that overwhelmingly won the day. It was a stark repudiation of revivalism's theology of conversion—and of the Holy Spirit's direct involvement.

So is it appropriate to call Cane Ridge America's Pentecost? I would say yes in view of its powerful shaping effect on American evangelical pietism. And I would say yes in view of the way it propelled Stone's "Christian" movement. But for Campbell's Disciples movement, it was nothing of the sort. It was an embarrassing and dangerous delusion.

In the concluding chapter, I will say more about why.

NOTES

[1]Conkin, *Cane Ridge*, 173.

[2]Letter from a Kentucky minister in *Increase of Piety, or the Revival of Religion in the United States of America* (Newburyport, CT, 1802), quoted by Conkin, *Cane Ridge*, 93–94.

[3]Schmidt, *Holy Fairs*.

[4]See Boles, *The Great Revival*.

[5]Roberts and Roberts, "Like Fire in Dry Stubble (Part I)," 148–58; Roberts "Like Fire in Dry Stubble (Part II)," 26–40.

[6]Roberts, "Like Fire in Dry Stubble (Part II)," 26–40; Roberts, "Early Tennessee and Kentucky Preachers."

[7]Stone, "Retrospect," 314–16.

[8]Stone, 86.

[9]See Edwards, *Religious Affections*, 197–239, and Wesley, *Fifty-Three Sermons*.

[10]Campbell, "Kingdom of the Clergy,"49–56; Barton Stone, "Union," 180; Campbell, "Reply on Union," 390.

[11]Campbell, "Christendom in its Dotage," 374. See also Campbell, "Reply to Mr. Waterman," 251.

[12]Campbell, "Letter to William Jones, No. VI," 353; Campbell, "The Confirmation of the Testimony," 8–14.

[13]Campbell, "Mr. Lynd on the Influence of the Holy Spirit," 410.

[14]Campbell, "An Address to the Readers of the Christian Baptist. No. IV," 148.

[15]For an example, see the story of B. F. Hall, in Allen, *Distant Voices*, 32–38.

CHAPTER EIGHT

Revivalism, the Holy Spirit, and Unity

JOHN MARK HICKS

Samuel Davies ministered to seven Presbyterian congregations north of Richmond, Virginia, in Hanover County. He was the leading representative of the First Great Awakening in Virginia. When he died at the age of thirty-seven in 1761, he was the fourth president of what came to be known as Princeton University.

Davies hosted communion festivals among his churches for over a decade in the 1740s–1750s. The communion festival was an opportunity for and means of revival, as communion was transfigured from a mere memory of Christ's death into an experience of Christ's presence.[1] Davies utilized it as a means of revival among his Presbyterian congregations. This included seating enslaved Africans at the table. Schmidt notes Davies's excitement when he testified in 1756, "I had the pleasure of seeing the table of the Lord adorned with about forty-four black faces."[2]

Davies's use of the table tended toward unity, and this is consistent with his famous sermon entitled "The Sacred Import of the Christian Name." He wrote, "Let us consider the Christian name, as a UNIVERSAL name, intended to bury all party denominations." Though Paul himself "took pains to crush the first risings of this party spirit," Davies's contemporaries fostered an "endless variety of denominations . . . derived from some leading men, or from some little theological peculiarities." He concluded his first point in the sermon with this blunt statement: "I am a Christian, a mere Christian! I have no other religion! My church is the Christian Church."[3] His ideas fed a stream of thought that later shaped Rice Haggard's influential pamphlet "An Address to the Different Religious Societies, on the Sacred Import of the Christian Name."[4] Barton W. Stone was part of the group that published Haggard's pamphlet in 1804.

One of Davies's students was David Caldwell, a New Light Presbyterian who served as both an educator and revivalist in North Carolina. He was one of Davies's pallbearers in 1761.[5] Stone attended Caldwell's Academy for three years from 1790 to 1793. In this way, Stone not only encountered the revivalism of New Light Presbyterianism but also the rather ecumenical and nondenominational spirit of Samuel Davies.

Revival of Unity

As Stone participated in the revivalism of the Second Great Awakening in 1801 Kentucky, he brought with him a broad sense of Christian unity. Newell Williams has argued that "Stone's experience of the Great Revival formed the view of our unity in Christ that he would bequeath to the Stone-Campbell Movement."[6] In fact, when Stone remembered Cane Ridge and the Great Revival some twenty-six years later, he enthusiastically regarded it not only as an evangelistic event but a revival of unity:

> The doctrine preached by all was simple, and nearly the same. Free and full salvation to every creature was proclaimed. All urged faith in the gospel, and obedience to it, as the way of life. All appeared deeply impressed with the ruined state of sinners, and were anxious for their salvation. The spirit of partyism, and party distinctions, were apparently forgotten. . . . The spirit of love, peace, and union, were revived. You might have seen the various sects engaged in the same spirit, praying, praising, and communing together, and the preachers in the lead. Happy days![7]

And this is no mere nostalgia on Stone's part. Two separate contemporary accounts also reflect this sense of excitement for unity and cooperation. The following was published in a paper soon after Cane Ridge. "Some, perhaps, will censure us for associating with the Baptists and Methodists: But, my dear Sir, we are all very friendly; there appears to be good doing; all are encouraging it; and is this not better, than to be devouring one another? Is it not more agreeable with the command of Christ, whose every precept is love?"[8] Another gentleman from Washington, Kentucky, wrote to his son about the Great Kentucky Revival on March 19, 1801, more than five months before Cane Ridge:

> The spirit of God appears in powerful operation among all denominations of Christians; "And if it was the Lord of the household's will, I would that all party names were united in that of Christians. And that the profession in the belief of one Lord, one Faith, one Baptism, one God and Father, might take place: that there might be but one visible household of Faith, that all might be of one heart, and one mind, and join hands in building up the torn down walls of Zion, which party zeal has

> almost demolished . . . the present revival of religion goes far, to unite the hearts of its professors."[9]

Stone learned in the Great Western Revivals that the work of the Spirit is not bounded by creedal confessions. Stone's early experiences at the sacramental meetings in 1801 encouraged the perspective that the Spirit works through the hearing of the gospel despite the creedal differences between preachers. He saw this in the revivals. "Many old and young, even little children, professed religion, and all declared the same simple gospel of Jesus. I knew the voice and felt the power."[10]

The Spirit of Unity

In the months after Cane Ridge, Stone and four others leaders formed the Springfield Presbytery, published Haggard's pamphlet, and then quickly dissolved the presbytery so that it might sink into the body of Christ at large. In their 1803 *Apology* for their actions, they wrote:

> But these human *aids* fail to attain the end designed by them, that is unity. For people soon begin to dispute as much about the meaning of their creeds, as about the Scriptures. And any unity which they do preserve, is like its source, human, barren, unsavory; not like that sweet union of soul, which is provided by the Spirit of God, living in his people. Indeed they are only sorry shifts to supply the want of "the unity of the Spirit, and bond of peace." Say, ye that love the Lord, what is it that unites you together? Is it a *creed,* or the living Spirit of the crucified Jesus?[11]

In the aftermath of the Great Kentucky Revival, this reference to the "living Spirit" points to the unity Stone envisioned.

Stone's vivid memories, his heighted sense of the Spirit's presence in the Great Revival, and his theological commitments stressed the role of the Spirit in uniting believers in the one body of Christ. Thirty years later, Stone recalled what he saw in evangelists from different denominations: "I saw them filled with the Holy Spirit of their Lord, addressing the multitudes, not in iceberg style, nor according to the studied rules of rhetoric and oratory; but in the language and spirit of heaven."[12]

In 1833, Stone recalled a common topic of his preaching during the first decade of the nineteenth century. He identified four types of unity. Book unity was founded on a creed. Head union was founded on a consensus of unwritten opinions. Water union was "founded on immersion into water." But Stone opted for "fire" union, which is the unity of the Spirit. The Spirit is "promised to those who obey" God and "leads" them "to love God and his children—to love and pray for all mankind." "In vain," Stone wrote, "we expect union without this spirit" because the Spirit is the "bond of union."[13]

A New Five-Finger Exercise

But what does this look like practically? How do we practice and embody this unity for the sake of our witness both to the truth of what God has done and to the unbelieving world? In answer to this question, and in conclusion, I suggest five (yes, count them, *five*) modes of visible unity that give expression to the underlying unity of the Spirit among believers. These practices not only exhibit the unity of the Spirit but are also means by which the Spirit dynamically works among believers for unity. At the same time, these practices are also transformative as they move us not only into a deeper experience and recognition of that unity but also function to transform us as exhibits of that unity.

First, confession: we confess Jesus is Lord by the Spirit. Paul provides the ground of this point: "No one is able to say 'Jesus is Lord' except by (in) the Holy Spirit" (1 Cor. 12:3). Contextually, this stands in contrast with those who say "Jesus is cursed" or who serve idols. This is our orienting confession. It is a centered-set confession—that is, we confess Jesus at the center of our faith journey. It confesses the direction to which we have turned our face; we walk toward Jesus in whom, by the Spirit, God is reconciling the world to the Triune God.

Second, transformation: we are sanctified by the Spirit (1 Thess. 4:3–8). Sanctification is a work that belongs to the Holy Spirit who indwells, empowers, and gifts us for new life in Christ. Stone stressed the importance of transformation in the life of the believer and as evidence of one's relationship to God. He recognized transformation as the work of the Spirit. Stone quotes Matthew 7:16 ("by their fruits you will know them") to make this point: "All were admitted to fellowship that believed in the Lord Jesus Christ, and obeyed him; and their obedience was considered the best evidence of their faith." This is, according to Stone, the "term of fellowship."[14] These first and second points are summarized by Stone in this way: "We are neither Pedo-Baptists, Arians nor Socianians; yet God forbid that we should reject or despise any of these little ones that believe in Jesus as an all-sufficient Saviour, and who proves the sincerity of his faith by a holy walk and conversation."[15]

Third, liturgy: we worship in the Spirit (John 4:24; Phil. 3:3). Liturgy was important for Stone as he recognized the value of assembly for transformation, education, and community. In particular, Stone was insistent on an open table, that is, all Christians are always welcome at the table of the Lord irrespective of their opinions, denominational affiliation, or immaturity. Hearing about revivals in the East in 1831, he offered this perspective: "I have read in an Eastern paper of the character of the revivals in one section of that country. It states that Christians of all denominations lovingly united in worship, even in the breaking of bread at the Lord's table. In such a work I will rejoice."[16] To recognize that the Spirit is the means by whom we commune with and experience God, and that this means is not dependent upon perfectionistic obedience to specified forms, and that the Spirit is not limited by forms, enables us to affirm the presence of the Spirit among those communities who do not share the forms that we think are most biblical. We may embrace the unity of believers (worshippers) through our eschatological and sacramental encounter with God in assembly by the enabling presence of the Spirit.

Fourth, practicing the kingdom of God: we minister in the power of the Spirit (Luke 4:18–19). The Spirit anointed Jesus, led him into the wilderness, and empowered him for ministry in Luke 3–4. This is the ministry of the kingdom of God where Jesus practiced the kingdom of God by heralding the good news of the kingdom, exercising authority over the principalities and powers, and healing brokenness. Jesus was sent, and he now sends a people empowered by the Spirit Whom God pours out generously on the church. Cooperation among believers in this mission is what Stone found so appealing in the Great Kentucky Revival. This is the missional ministry into which believers are called. This praxis is an expression of the life of the Spirit within the community because the community of Jesus empowered by the Spirit continues the teaching and doing of Jesus—that is, they continue to practice the kingdom of God.

Fifth, spiritual formation practices: we pray in the Spirit (Jude 20). Stone cultivated a deeper experience of prayer in his movement. He regarded prayer as that which offers a "habitual sense of the presence and inspection of God, and of our entire dependence upon him, which is the foundation of a holy life." This presence is "direct and immediate." In fact, "the denial of the direct operation of the Spirit cuts the very nerves of prayer," and, Stone continued:

> We can conceive of no doctrine more dangerous to the souls of men, than that, which tends to check and destroy the spirit of prayer. Prayer is the means by which we receive the grace of God, and enjoy sacred communion with the Father and the son. Enjoying this we have communion one with another, and grow up into Christ our living head in all things.[17]

Our present experience of visible unity is always in process. The present is not a perfect manifestation of the eschatological *telos* (or goal). Consequently, we pursue unity, just as we pursue sanctification. Though we have not yet experienced the fullness of our unity with God and with each other, we do experience that future when we give space to the presence of the Spirit. Since we are already united in the Spirit, we progressively manifest and experience that reality as the Spirit sanctifies our communities and our lives. Visible unity is a process of communal sanctification.

Through the practice of the above gifts, the Spirit mediates a proleptic experience of that eschatological unity. Together, we confess Jesus is Lord; together, we seek transformation; together, we participate in the eschatological assembly around the throne of God; together, we practice the kingdom of God; and together, we pray in the Spirit. Yes, you counted correctly. The number is five.

NOTES

[1]Clary, "Holy Communion and Revivalism in the First Great Awakening," 100–111.

[2]Schmidt, *Holy Fairs*, 57.

[3]Davies, *Important Subjects*, 1:215, 218.

[4] Haggard, *An Address to the Different Religious Societies.*

[5] Caldwell, *Dr. David Caldwell*, 19.

[6] Williams, "Our Unity in Christ," 44.

[7] Stone, "History of the Christian Church, No. I," 77. See the Appendix.

[8] Woodward, ed., "Extract from a Paper Published in Lancaster," 229.

[9] Woodword, ed., "Extract of a Letter from a Gentleman in Washington, KY," 47.

[10] Stone, *A Reply to John P. Campbell's Strictures*, 6.

[11] Stone, Marshall, Dunlavy, M'Nemar, and Thompson, *An Apology for Renouncing the Jurisdiction of the Synod of Kentucky*, 233.

[12] Stone, "Revivals of Religion," 164. See the Appendix.

[13] Stone, "Retrospect," 314–16.

[14] Stone, "Objections to Christian Union Calmly Considered," 27.

[15] Stone, "To the Editors of the Baptist Recorder," 225.

[16] Stone, "Revivals of Religion," 165.

[17] Stone, "On Prayer," 235–36.

CHAPTER NINE

The Eclipse of Cane Ridge in the Restoration Movement

LEONARD ALLEN

The Aura of Cane Ridge

From its beginning in 1804, Barton Stone's New Light "Christian" movement was infused with the aura of Cane Ridge. As we saw earlier, some of the exercises—holy singing especially—continued as regular features of worship in some Stoneite churches, and for a good while conversions tended to follow the revivalistic pattern. Stone continued to view conversion as a profound spiritual transformation wrought in the believer by the convicting power of the Holy Spirit. He shared John Wesley's view of "the testimony of the Spirit as an inward impression on the soul, whereby the Spirit of God directly 'witnesses to my spirit that I am a child of God.'" And, like Wesley, Stone was careful to correlate the Spirit's inward witness with the Spirit's genuine fruit—that is, with what Wesley called "inward and outward holiness."[1] As we have seen, Stone always looked favorably on revivalism and, as late as 1832, was willing to retain the mourner's bench, which was a symbol and tool of camp-meeting-type conversions.

Cane Ridge also left Stone with a passion for the unity of Christians and for freedom in the Spirit. The intense and practical spirit of unity he experienced in the revival Stone tied to the outpouring of the Spirit. The conversions, the exercises, and the stunning display of unity were all tied together. They could only be explained by the Spirit's fire. We can also say that the Spirit's fire lit in Stone a passion for freedom from the theological intricacies of human creeds and the constriction of human traditions, and a passion for restoration of simple New Testament Christianity.

This was the aura of Cane Ridge that pervaded the Stoneite churches as they steadily spread throughout the Cumberland region, mostly in the backwoods.

But in 1823 a new voice appeared in Kentucky. Alexander Campbell came to Kentucky to debate the Presbyterian W. L. McCalla on the topic of baptism. Campbell's argument about the role of baptism for remission—and the new pattern of conversion (*ordo salutis*) it anchored—quickly resonated with thousands of Stoneite Christians in the region. Campbell's precise "ancient gospel" provided theological structure, rational certainty, and blessed assurance for many whose experiential conversions had left them unsure of where they stood with God. And his simple outline of the "ancient order of things" gave primitive Christianity a new clarity and structure.

The Stoneite "Christians" gradually adopted Campbell's new theology of conversion and church order. As this change happened, the movement underwent an unforeseen but major transformation. As the "Christian" movement converged with Campbell's "current reformation" (in the 1830s and beyond), the aura of Cane Ridge receded. Indeed, it was mostly eclipsed by

Campbell's Old Light sensibilities, his new *ordo salutis,* and his Baconian rationalism. When Campbell's "Disciples" and Stone's "Christians" formally united in January 1832, the handwriting was already on the wall: the theology and practices of Cane Ridge and the Great Revival would be quickly eclipsed and left behind in the new "Stone-Campbell movement."

Three Strikes

There were three strikes against Cane Ridge and what it stood for. Strike one, as we saw in a previous chapter, was Campbell's Old Light or anti-revival sensibilities, which were deep in his bones. Strike two was his new pattern of conversion which completely removed the direct operation of the Spirit from the conversion process. For Campbell, conversion did not involve, as in classical Protestantism, a direct work of the Spirit to convict of sin, to infuse faith as a gift, and to produce a deep change of affections. Rather, for Campbell conversion involved an unbreakable chain of cause and effect: "gospel facts," testimony to those facts, belief of the testimony, obeying the gospel, then appropriate feelings or "affections." When converted, one entered a new state or legal standing before God—change of affections then gradually followed acceptance of the "gospel facts." Campbell, in short, rationalized conversion, turning it into an ordered, educational process that followed certain inviolable natural laws.[2]

In the years that followed the union of the two movements, Stone came to believe that something was missing from Campbell's pattern of conversion. After he had witnessed this rational, quick, and orderly pattern of conversion at work for fifteen or twenty years, Stone expressed strong concerns. He had no doubt that, for believers who languished under conviction of sin, the call simply to "obey the gospel" upon a profession of faith was a great balm. It had opened the door to gospel assurance and peace for many people. But he believed that it also had short-circuited the process of repentance and swept people into the church who had not experienced deep sorrow for sin and true heart change. The result, he thought, was a widespread spirit of coldness and nominalism in the churches.

Strike three against the theological legacy of Cane Ridge was Campbell's embrace of the Lockean philosophy (often called the "Baconian Philosophy" in the nineteenth century) as a tool to oppose revivalism and to set forth his view of conversion and the Holy Spirit.

God's power to affect people, Campbell said many times, is "all contained in [revealed] words." The Bible already "contains all the arguments which can be offered to reconcile man to God, and to purify them who are reconciled," and therefore "all the power of the Holy Spirit which can operate on the human mind is spent."[3] To be filled with the Spirit thus meant little more than having the words and arguments of the Bible in one's mind. And in regard to prayer's petitions, one must not expect supernatural aid or that the laws of nature would be changed, suspended, or modified by our requests. Here was a doctrine of the Spirit newly minted in the modern period.

This philosophical framework was strike three. Cane Ridge was out.

The "Moral" Power of Biblical Words

Campbell removed the direct work of the Spirit entirely from conversion, and though he didn't mean to remove the direct work of the Spirit entirely from the post-conversion life of Christians, that was a strong effect in the tradition he created.

Beginning in the 1840s Campbell's younger colleague and friend, Robert Richardson, saw this tendency clearly. Limiting the Spirit's influence to the Bible alone, he said, "degrades the

Bible by placing it in a false position, and ascribing to it exclusive power and attributes which it never claims for itself." In 1843 he urged Mr. Campbell not to defend (in his upcoming debate with N. L. Rice) the proposition that "in conversion and sanctification the Spirit works only through the word of truth."[4] But Campbell did defend it.

Fourteen years later, after many years of mounting concern, Richardson took on Tolbert Fanning, editor of the *Gospel Advocate*, over the matter of the Spirit and the Christian life. Since Richardson could not or would not take on his friend Alexander Campbell directly,[5] he chose Fanning as a kind of stand-in since Fanning had embraced Campbell's "Word only" stance aggressively. Such a view of the Spirit, Richardson stated, strikes at the heart of Christian faith, distorting its nature, sapping it power, and diminishing its enjoyment. Because it "constantly seeks to resolve everything into . . . mere words," the effect of this doctrine is "to unfit men's minds to receive anything that is not merely outward and formal," and thus it is "naturally and directly antagonistic to everything spiritual in religion."[6] The practical effect was spiritual debilitation.

The issue at stake between Richardson and Fanning (and Campbell) was precisely this: does the Spirit guide, comfort, empower, and sustain Christians through means other than biblical words? Fanning said no. Campbell said no much of the time. Richardson said yes and amen. Stone would have answered, "Where in the world did you even come up with that idea?"

I have argued that this obscure 1857 exchange between Richardson and Fanning represents a kind of crossroads in the history of Churches of Christ,[7] and to a lesser extent among those who became the Christian Churches and Churches of Christ. The Campbell and Fanning path remained dominant, and Richardson's path continued to be a way less traveled.

The sharp difference in Stone and Campbell's view of divine agency can be seen clearly in the issue of miracles. Stone remained open all of his life to God's direct, even "miraculous," working in the world, while Campbell taught that God worked presently only through secondary channels like natural law and the Bible. "I see no authority in scripture," Stone wrote in an open letter to Walter Scott in the 1830s, "why we should draw the conclusion, that the miraculous gift of the Holy Spirit, is, according to the will of God, withdrawn from the church."[8]

Alexander Campbell, in contrast, emphatically rejected any place for miracles in the modern world, and this view became uniform in the tradition that followed. Once miracles had validated the Bible as God's Word and testified to the founding events of the Christian church their role was complete. Since that time God worked only through natural law and the "moral" power of words in the Bible.

Stone's Legacy

Among the emerging nineteenth-century Churches of Christ, the memory of Barton Stone and Cane Ridge faded quickly.[9] But Stone's legacy continued—though without his name—in the career of David Lipscomb and James Harding. Though Lipscomb and Harding imbibed much of Campbell's rational and common sense theology, they also reveal some continuity with Stone.[10] They promoted a dynamic vision of God's inbreaking kingdom which one day would fill the earth. They called for a countercultural lifestyle, for dependence upon God's "miraculous" providence and indwelling Spirit, for the spiritual disciplines of prayer, Bible reading, and caring for the poor, and for disciples to back away from patriotism which was often idolatrous.[11]

James Harding especially believed that the Holy Spirit was a vital, direct, and active presence in the life of Christians. We hunger for intimacy with God and for deep transformation, he believed, and it is through the indwelling Spirit that we experience this. The Spirit helps our infirmities. "A book cannot pray or groan" on our behalf; only the Spirit can do that. "I am as far as the East is from the West," said Harding, "from believing that neither God, Christ, nor the Holy Spirit can help us except by talking to us."[12] Harding thought the "Word only" view was a deadly doctrine: "I do not know any doctrine taught by any of the Protestant sectarian bodies that is more flatly contradictory of the general tenor of Scripture, that is a more blighting, withering, deadly curse to those who believe it."[13]

Harding's passionate advocacy of a strong doctrine of God's providence and God's active Spirit exerted considerable influence between 1890 and 1917. He died in 1922, and his view of the Spirit and providence was quickly eclipsed. Campbell's (and Fanning's) "Word only" doctrine continued its dominance, propelled to new heights in the early twentieth century by the strong polemics of R. L. Whiteside and his protégé, Foy E. Wallace Jr.[14]

Renewing the Doctrine of the Spirit

In my typology of five major Holy Spirit traditions in Christian history, I placed Churches of Christ/Stone-Campbell churches in the Modernist tradition.[15] Modernist views of the Spirit arose as stress fell more and more upon the "reasonableness of Christianity" (John Locke). Alexander Campbell partook of this spirit and wove it into the fabric of his restoration movement. It's the garment in which we were clothed. But after modernity, it doesn't wear so well.

I dare say that some (maybe most) of us, if we had been at Cane Ridge, would have found ourselves way past our Campbellite comfort zones. Like Campbell, some of us would have abhorred it, convinced that such behavior discredits the gospel to people of reason. But whatever one's taste or distaste for the revival, let me suggest that the Cane Ridge communion festival might be more than a fascinating historical curiosity of the early Stone-Campbell movement. Cane Ridge, of course, bore the unique marks of its own time and its own particular setting. But here I suggest that it can provoke and stir us toward the needed recovery of a more biblical, missional doctrine of the Spirit. It can bear witness, if we will let it, to the fresh, surprising, and sometimes strange work of God the Spirit.

The doctrine of the Spirit is being renewed in our time. No longer is it the stepchild of theology. In *Poured Out*, I set out five reasons why. One basic reason is the collapse of Christendom in the West and the growing sense that Christians are on mission in a new, more hostile environment. The Spirit is the power of God's mission, and Christians are being forced to come to terms with their mission in new ways. They are becoming more aware that they need the Spirit's empowerment to live on God's mission.[16]

I close with four brief affirmations about the Spirit of God that point us toward a more robust, biblical, and missional doctrine of the Spirit.[17] First, the Holy Spirit is not a junior member of the Trinity. Indeed, I put forth the claim that the role or mission of the Spirit is equal in importance to the mission of Jesus the Son. The two missions are distinct but deeply intertwined.

Second, the Holy Spirit is the power of God's inbreaking reign or kingdom. Permeating the New Testament is the claim that disciples of Jesus live in the overlap of two ages: this present age and the age to come, the "already" and the "not yet." The Spirit is the presence and power of this inbreaking age to come. The diminishment or loss of this sense of the Spirit's inbreaking has big consequences for the church and its mission.

Third, the Holy Spirit is no tame spirit—not the "shy member" of the Trinity. The Spirit of God presses the people of God relentlessly toward "new creation," shaking up the status quo, bestowing "power from on high," aiding the putting-to-death process in the untransformed places of our lives, and "groaning" with us as we join with the groaning creation.

Fourth, the Holy Spirit, as the Nicene Creed says, is the "giver of life," the Spirit of resurrection and new life. To be filled with this Spirit is to be lifted up out of apathy, brokenness, cynicism, even despair, and to become fruitful again. As in Ezekiel's vision of the dry bones, the Spirit comes like a wind from the four corners of the earth to bring new life (Ezek. 37:1–14).

Surely we can agree that in our increasingly post-Christian culture we need more of the Spirit's power in order to be faithful disciples, to be God's "royal priesthood" in the mending of a broken and still groaning creation. But openness to the Spirit is risky, for the Spirit is no shy or tame Spirit. "Does this make you nervous?" Roger Olson asks. "It should. The Holy Spirit is not predictable or safe. The Holy Spirit shatters the status quo, breaking us out of complacency and lifting us up to new heights of spiritual fullness and blessing—if we are open to that."[18]

NOTES

[1]Wesley, "The Witness of the Spirit" (1746). See Bevins, "The Historical Development of Wesley's Doctrine of the Spirit," 161–81.

[2]On Campbell's discovery and articulation of the "ancient gospel" as a reaction to the revivalistic pattern of conversion, see Allen, *Things Unseen*, 45–50.

[3]Campbell, "Dialogue on the Holy Spirit—Part 1," 295–96; "Dialogue on the Holy Spirit—Part 2," 369; "Incidents on a Tour to Nashville, TN. No. 1," 560; "Prayer—No. 1," 471.

[4]Smith, *Alexander Campbell*, 328.

[5]But Richardson did speak bluntly about Mr. Campbell in private correspondence. "The philosophy of Locke with which Bro. Campbell's mind was deeply imbued in youth," he wrote to Isaac Errett on July 16, 1857, "has insidiously mingled itself with almost all the great points in the reformation and has been all the while like an iceberg in the way—chilling the heart and

numbing the hands, and impeding all progress in the right direction." Cited by Goodnight and Stevenson, *Home to Bethphage*, 123.

[6] Richardson, "Faith vs. Philosophy—No. 5," 329. For a full treatment of this episode, see Allen, "Unearthing the 'Dirt Philosophy,'" 71–98.

[7] See Allen and Swick, *Participating in God's Life*.

[8] Stone, "Letter to Walter Scott," 13–14.

[9] See Allen, "The Stone That the Builders Rejected," in *Things Unseen*, 99–116.

[10] See Hughes, "The Apocalyptic Origins of Churches of Christ," 181–214.

[11] See Hicks and Valentine, *Kingdom Come*.

[12] Harding, "How Does God Help His People?" 9.

[13] Harding, "Atlanta—God's Providence—The Holy Spirit," 9; Harding, "God's Churches versus Man's Societies, No. II," 8.

[14] See Valentine, "Robertson Lafayette Whiteside."

[15] Allen, *Poured Out*, 46–48.

[16] Allen, *Poured Out*, 24–28.

[17] These points are adapted from Allen, *Poured Out*, 6.

[18] Olson, "A Pentecost Sermon: The Holy Spirit."

APPENDIX

Cane Ridge in the Original Sources

1. Rev. George Addison Baxter on the Cane Ridge Revival (1802)

Excerpt from Woodward, *Surprising Accounts of the Revival of Religion* (1802), 106–09

Introduction

On January 1, 1802, Rev. George Addison Baxter, the Principal of Washington Academy (now Washington and Lee University) in Lexington, Virginia, wrote a letter to Rev. Dr. Archibald Alexander, the President of Hampden-Sydney College in Hampden Sydney, Virginia. Alexander would later become the first professor to serve at Princeton Theological Seminary, which began in 1812. Baxter describes the sacramental character of the Cane Ridge meeting and how revivalism was an antidote to Deism, whose skepticism threatened the faith of many as it did in the early days of Alexander's own faith journey. The letter assures Alexander, who believed God uses seasons of revival, that the Kentucky revival is authentic.

Excerpt

Its [the revival's] influence was not less visible in promoting a friendly temper; nothing could appear more amiable than that undissembled benevolence which governs the subjects of this work: I have often wished that the mere politician or Deist could observe with impartiality their peaceful and amicable spirit. He would certainly see that nothing could equal the religion of JESUS, for promoting even the temporal happiness of society—some neighbourhoods visited by the revival had been formerly notorious for private animosities; and many petty law-suits had commenced on that ground. When the parties in these quarrels were impressed with religion, the first thing was to send for their antagonists; and it was often very affecting to see their meeting. Both had seen their faults, and both contended that they ought to make concessions, till at last they were obliged to request each other to forbear all mention of the past, and to act as friends and brothers for the future. Now sir, let modern philosophists talk of reforming the world by banishing Christianity and introducing their licentious systems. The blessed gospel of our God and Saviour is shewing what it can do.

Some circumstances have concurred to distinguish the Kentucky revival from most others, of which we have had any account, I mean the largeness of the assemblies on sacramental occasions. The length of time, they continued on the ground in devotional exercises. And the great numbers who have fallen down under religious impressions,—on each of these particulars I shall make some remarks.

With respect to the largeness of the assemblies. It is generally supposed that at many places there were not fewer than 8,

10, or 12 thousand people—at a place called Cane Ridge meeting-house, many are of opinion there were at least 20 thousand. There were 140 wagons which came loaded with people, besides other wheel carriages. Some persons had come 200 miles. The largeness of these assemblies was an inconvenience—they were too numerous to be addressed by one speaker, it therefore became necessary for several ministers to officiate at the same time at different stands: this afforded an opportunity to those who were but slightly impressed with religion to wander to and fro between the different places of worship, which created an appearance of confusion and gave ground to such as were unfriendly to the work to charge it with disorder. Another cause also conduced to the same effect; about this time the people began to fall down in great numbers under serious impressions: this was a new thing among Presbyterians; it excited universal astonishment, and created a curiosity which could not be restrained when people FELL even during the most solemn parts of divine service: those who stood near were so extremely anxious to see how they were affected, that they often crowded about them so as to disturb the worship. —But these causes of disorder were soon removed; different sacraments were appointed on the same Sabbath, which divided the people, and the falling down became so familiar as to excite no disturbance.

In October I attended three Sacraments, at each there were supposed to be 4 or 5 thousand people, and everything was conducted with strict propriety; when persons fell, those who were near took care of them, and everything continued quiet until the worship was concluded.

The length of time that people continue at the places of worship is another important circumstance of the Kentucky revival: at Cane Ridge they met on Friday and continued until Wednesday evening, night and day without intermission, either in the public or private exercises of devotion; and with such earnestness that heavy showers of rain were not sufficient to disperse them. On other Sacramental occasions they generally continued on the ground until Monday or Tuesday evening; and had not the preachers been exhausted and obliged to retire or had they chosen to prolong the worship, they might have kept the people any length of time they pleased, and all this was, or might have been done, in a country where less than twelve months before the Clergy found it difficult to detain the people during the usual exercises of the Sabbath. The practice of camping on the ground was introduced, partly by necessity, and partly by inclination; the assemblies were generally too large to be received by any common neighbourhood; everything indeed was done which hospitality and brotherly kindness could do, to accommodate the people; public and private houses were opened, and free invitations given to all persons who wished to retire. Farmers gave up their meadows before they were mown to supply the horses; yet notwithstanding all this liberality it would have been impossible in many cases, to have accommodated the whole assemblies with private lodgings: but besides the people were unwilling to suffer any interruption in their devotions; and they formed an attachment to the place where they were continually seeing so many careless sinners receiving their first impressions, and so many Deists constrained to call on the formerly despised name of JESUS; they conceived a sentiment like what Jacob felt at Bethel. "Surely the Lord is in this place," "This is none other but the house of God, and this is the gate of Heaven."

The number of persons who have fallen down under serious impressions in this revival, is another matter worthy of attention, and on this I shall be more particular, as it seems to be the principal cause why this work should be more suspected of enthusiasm than some other revivals.

At Cane Ridge sacrament it is generally supposed not less than 1000 persons fell prostrate to the ground; among whom were many infidels. At one sacrament which I attended, the number that fell was thought to be more than 300. Persons who fall, are generally such as had manifested symptoms of the deepest impressions for some time previous to that event. It is common to see them shed tears plentifully for about an hour.

Questions for Engagement

1. Why is Baxter so eager to communicate about the Cane Ridge Revival with Alexander?

2. What sorts of religious exercises does he recount, and what is his assessment of them?

3. In what ways, according to Baxter, did Cane Ridge excel as an exemplar of revivalism?

2. Letter from a Brother to His Sister about the Cane Ridge Revival (1801)

Excerpt from Woodward, *Surprising Accounts of the Revival of Religion*, 57–58.

Introduction

Both the author and the addressee are unknown, but the brother lived in Lexington, Kentucky, and his sister lived in Philadelphia, Pennsylvania. The letter is dated August 10, 1801. This firsthand account of the Cane Ridge Revival reveals its diverse nature as well its sacramental practices.

Excerpt

Dear Sister,

I hasten to give you an account of the revival of religion, and some of the remarkable circumstances thereof. I am sure the most discerning and observant pensman, or the nicest pencil, could not portray to your imagination, the full idea of the meeting that took place at Kain-ridge, in Bourbon-county:—I shall confine myself only to a few particulars—"This meeting was published about one month generally, throughout the Presbyterian connexion, as one of their annual sacraments: thither assembled the religious of every denomination, some from one hundred miles distant, but more particularly the Presbyterians and Methodists, who are in full communion with each other:—lastly the Baptists, who preach with each other, but do not commune. To this general assembly I set off last Friday, and arrived there on Saturday about 10 o'clock: I then began to note some of the most extraordinary particulars:

I first proceeded to count the waggons containing families, with their provisions, camp equipage, &c. to the number of 147: at 11 o'clock the quantity of ground occupied by horses, waggons, &c. was about the same size as the square between Market, Chesnut, Second and Third-streets, of Philadelphia—There was at this place a stage erected in the woods, about 100 yards from the meeting-house, where were a number of Presbyterian and Methodist ministers; one of the former preaching to as many as could get near enough to hear—in the house also, was another of the same denomination, preaching to a crowded audience—at the same time another large concourse of people collected about 100 yards in an east direction from the meeting-house, hearing a Methodist speaker—and about 150 yards in a fourth course from the house was an assembly of black people, hearing the exhortations of the blacks, some of whom appeared deeply convicted, and others converted. The number of communicants who received tokens were 750, nor was there a sufficiency of them—these tokens are small pieces of lead, the size of a five-penny bit, with the letter A or B impressed thereon, and distributed by the ministers to the members of the several churches, not excluding any baptist who apply for them. I believe there was at one time as many as three hundred who exhorted on this occasion. I noted a remarkable instance of a little girl, by the name of Barbara, about 7 years old, who was set upon a man's shoulder, agreeably to her desire, to speak to the multitude, which she did, until she appeared almost exhausted, and leaned back her head on her bearer. A tender hearted old man, standing close behind her, observed, "Poor thing, she had better be laid down;" at which she quickly turned round her head, and said, "Don't call me poor, for Christ is my brother, God my father, and I have a kingdom to inherit, therefore don't call me poor, for I am rich in the blood of the Lamb."

Questions for Engagement

1. What sort of diversity is present at Cane Ridge?

2. What can you learn about Presbyterian sacramental practices from this excerpt?

3. Barton Stone's Observation of Religious Exercises and Argument for Their Legitimacy (1844)

Excerpt from Stone, *The Biography of Eld. Barton Warren Stone*, 34–38.

Introduction

Forty years later, Barton Stone described the religious exercises he observed in revivals under James McGready in southern Kentucky in 1801. Directly after Stone's return to northern Kentucky, the exercises emerged in Stone's congregations and, most notably, at the Cane Ridge Revival in August 1801. In this excerpt, Stone emphasizes both the legitimacy and purpose of the extraordinary religious exercises and the free-will message he preached at the time.

Excerpt

Things moved on quietly in my congregations, and in the country generally. Apathy in religious societies appeared every where to an alarming degree. Not only the power of religion had disappeared, but also the very form of it was waning fast away, and continued so till the beginning of the present century. Having heard of a remarkable religious excitement in the south of Kentucky, and in Tennessee, under the labors of James McGready and other Presbyterian ministers, I was very anxious to be among them; and, early in the spring of 1801, went there to attend a camp-meeting. There, on the edge of a prairie in Logan county, Kentucky, the multitudes came together, and continued a number of days and nights encamped on the ground; during which time worship was carried on in some part of the encampment. The scene to me was new, and passing strange. It baffled description. Many, very many fell down, as men slain in battle, and continued for hours together in an apparently breathless and motionless state—sometimes for a few moments reviving, and exhibiting symptoms of life by a deep groan, or piercing shriek, or by a prayer for mercy most fervently uttered. After lying thus for hours, they obtained deliverance. The gloomy cloud, which had covered their faces, seemed gradually and visibly to disappear, and hope in smiles brightened into joy—they would rise shouting deliverance, and then would address the surrounding multitude in language truly eloquent and impressive. With astonishment did I hear men, women and children declaring the wonderful works of God, and the glorious mysteries of the gospel. Their appeals were solemn, heart-penetrating, bold and free. Under such addresses many others would fall down into the same state from which the speakers had just been delivered.

Two or three of my particular acquaintances from a distance were struck down. I sat patiently by one of them, whom I knew to be a careless sinner, for hours, and observed with critical attention every thing that passed from the beginning to the end. I noticed the momentary revivings as from death—the humble confession of sins—the fervent prayer, and the ultimate deliverance—then the solemn thanks and praise to God—the affectionate exhortation to companions and to the people around, to repent and come to Jesus. I was astonished at the knowledge of gospel truth displayed in the address. The effect was, that several sunk down into the same appearance of death. After attending to many such cases, my conviction was complete that it was a good work—the work of God; nor has my mind wavered since on the subject. Much did I then see, and much have I since seen, that I considered to be fanaticism; but this should not condemn the work. The Devil has always tried to ape the works of God, to bring them into disrepute. But that cannot be a Satanic work, which brings men to humble confession and forsaking of sin—to solemn prayer—fervent praise and thanksgiving, and to sincere and affectionate exhortations to sinners to repent and go to Jesus the Saviour.

I am always hurt to hear people speak lightly of this work. I always think they speak of what they know nothing about. Should every thing bearing the impress of imperfection be blasphemously rejected, who amongst us at this time could stand? But more on this subject hereafter.

The meeting being closed, I returned with ardent spirits to my congregations. I reached my appointment at Caneridge on the Lord's-day. Multitudes had collected, anxious to hear the religious news of the meeting I had attended in Logan. I ascended the pulpit, and gave a relation of what I had seen and heard; then opened my Bible and preached from these words: "Go ye into all the world and preach the gospel to every creature. He that believeth and is baptized shall be saved, and he that believeth not shall be damned." On the universality of the gospel, and faith as the condition of salvation, I principally dwelt, and urged the sinner to believe now, and be saved. I labored to remove their pleas and objections, nor was it labor in vain. The congregation was affected with awful solemnity, and many returned home weeping. Having left appointments to preach in the congregation within a few days, I hurried over to Concord to preach at night. At our night meeting at Concord, two little girls were struck down under the preaching of the word, and in every respect were exercised as those were in the south of Kentucky, as already described. Their addresses made deep impressions on the congregation.

On the next day I returned to Caneridge, and attended my appointment at William Maxwell's. I soon heard of the good effects of the meeting on the Sunday before. Many were solemnly engaged in seeking salvation, and some had found the Lord, and were rejoicing in him. Among these last was my particular friend Nathaniel Rogers, a man of first respectability and influence in the neighborhood. Just as I arrived at the gate, my friend Rogers and his lady came up; as soon as he saw me, he shouted aloud the praises of God. We hurried into each others' embrace, he still praising the Lord aloud. The crowd left the house, and hurried to this novel scene. In less than twenty minutes, scores had fallen to the ground—paleness, trembling, and anxiety appeared in all—some attempted to fly from the scene panic stricken, but they either fell, or returned immediately to the crowd, as unable to get away. In the midst of this exercise, an intelligent deist in the neighborhood, stepped up to me, and said, Mr. Stone, I always thought before that you were an honest man; but now I am convinced you are deceiving the people. I viewed him with pity, and mildly spoke a few words to him—immediately he fell as a dead man, and rose no more till he confessed the Saviour. The meeting continued on that spot in the open air, till late at night, and many found peace in the Lord.

The effects of this meeting through the country were like fire in dry stubble driven by a strong wind. All felt its influence more or less. Soon after, we had a protracted meeting at Concord. The whole country appeared to be in motion to the place, and multitudes of all denominations attended. All seemed heartily to unite in the work, and in Christian love. Party spirit, abashed, shrunk away. To give a true description of this meeting cannot be done; it would border on the marvellous. It continued five days and nights without ceasing. Many, very many will through eternity remember it with thanksgiving and praise. . . .

This memorable meeting [at Cane Ridge] came on Thursday or Friday before the third Lord's-day in August, 1801. The roads were literally crowded with waggons, carriages, horsemen, and footmen, moving to the solemn camp. The sight was affecting. It was judged, by military men on the ground, that there were between twenty and thirty thousand collected. Four or five preachers were frequently speaking at the same time, in different parts of the encampment, without confusion. The Methodist and Baptist preachers aided in the work, and all appeared cordially united in it—of one mind and one soul, and the salvation of sinners seemed to be the great object of all. We all engaged in singing the same songs of praise—all united in prayer—all preached the same things—free salvation urged upon all by faith and repentance. A particular description of this meeting would fill a large volume, and then the half would not be told. The numbers converted will be known only in eternity. Many things transpired there, which were so much like miracles, that if they were not, they had the same effects as miracles on infidels and unbelievers; for many of them by these were convinced that Jesus was the Christ, and bowed in submission to him. This meeting continued six or seven days and nights, and would have continued longer, but provisions for such a multitude failed in the neighborhood.

To this meeting many had come from Ohio and other distant parts, who returned home and diffused the same spirit in their neighborhoods, and the same works followed. So low had religion sunk, and such carelessness universally had prevailed, that I have thought that nothing common could have arrested the attention of the world; therefore these uncommon agitations were sent for this purpose. . . .

Question for Engagement

1. Summarize Stone's case for the legitimacy and purpose of the "exercises."

4. Barton Stone on Religious Exercises (1844)

Excerpt from Stone, *The Biography of Eld. Barton Warren Stone*, 39–42

Introduction

In his autobiography, written forty years after the Great Revival in the West (1797–1805), which marked the beginnings of what historians call the Second Great Awakening, Barton Stone described seven religious exercises he had observed at the revivals in Kentucky. This excerpt includes Stone's description of the famous exercises. Even at the end of his life, he continued to believe the exercises must have been the mysterious work of God.

Excerpt

The bodily agitations or exercises, attending the excitement in the beginning of this century, were various, and called by various names. . . . The falling exercise was very common among all classes, the saints and sinners of every age and of every grade, from the philosopher to the clown. The subject of this exercise would, generally, with a piercing scream, fall like a log on the floor, earth, or mud, and appear as dead. Of thousands of similar cases, I will mention one. At a meeting, two gay young ladies, sisters, were standing together attending to the exercises and preaching at the time. Instantly they both fell, with a shriek of distress, and lay for more than an hour apparently in a lifeless state. Their mother, a pious Baptist, was in great distress, fearing they would not revive. At length they began to exhibit symptoms of life, by crying fervently for mercy, and then relapsed into the same death-like state, with an awful gloom on their countenances. After awhile, the gloom on the face of one was succeeded by a heavenly smile, and she cried out, precious Jesus, and rose up and spoke of the love of God—the preciousness of Jesus, and of the glory of the gospel, to the surrounding crowd, in language almost superhuman, and pathetically exhorted all to repentance. In a little while after, the other sister was similarly exercised. From that time they became remarkably pious members of the church. . . .

The jerks cannot be so easily described. Sometimes the subject of the jerks would be affected in some one member of the body, and sometimes in the whole system. When the head alone was affected, it would be jerked backward and forward, or from side to side, so quickly that the features of the face could not be distinguished. When the whole system was affected, I have seen the person stand in one place, and jerk backward and forward in quick succession, their head nearly touching the floor behind and before. All classes, saints and sinners, the strong as well as the weak, were thus affected. I have inquired of those thus affected. They could not account for it; but some have told me that those were among the happiest seasons of their lives. I have seen some wicked persons thus affected, and all the time cursing the jerks, while they were thrown to the earth with violence. Though so awful to behold, I do not remember that any one of the thousands I have seen ever sustained an injury in body. This was as strange as the exercise itself.

The dancing exercise. This generally began with the jerks, and was peculiar to professors of religion. The subject, after jerking awhile, began to dance, and then the jerks would cease. Such dancing was indeed heavenly to the spectators; there was nothing in it like levity, nor calculated to excite levity in the beholders. The smile of heaven shone on the countenance of the subject, and assimilated to angels appeared the whole person. Sometimes the motion was quick and sometimes slow. Thus they continued to move forward and backward in the same track or alley till nature seemed exhausted, and they would fall prostrate on the floor or earth, unless caught by those standing by. While thus exercised, I have heard their solemn praises and prayers ascending to God.

The barking exercise (as opposers contemptuously called it), was nothing but the jerks. A person affected with the jerks, especially in his head, would often make a grunt, or bark, if you please, from the suddenness of the jerk. This name of barking seems to have had its origin from an old Presbyterian preacher of East Tennessee. He had gone into the woods for private devotion, and was seized with the jerks. Standing near a sapling, he caught hold of it, to prevent his falling, and as his head jerked back, he uttered a grunt or kind of noise similar to a bark, his face being turned upwards. Some wag discovered him in this position, and reported that he found him barking up a tree.

The laughing exercise was frequent, confined solely with the religious. It was a loud, hearty laughter, but one *sui generis*; it excited laughter in none else. The subject appeared rapturously solemn, and his laughter excited solemnity in saints and sinners. It is truly indescribable.

The running exercise was nothing more than, that persons feeling something of these bodily agitations, through fear, attempted to run away, and thus escape from them; but it commonly happened that they ran not far, before they fell, or became so greatly agitated that they could proceed no farther. I knew a young physician of a celebrated family, who came some distance to a big meeting to see the strange things he had heard of. He and a young lady had sportively agreed to watch over, and take care of each other, if either should fall. At length the physician felt something very uncommon, and started from the congregation to run into the woods; he was discovered running as for life, but did not proceed far till he fell down, and there lay till he submitted to the Lord, and afterwards became a zealous member of the church. Such cases were common.

I shall close this chapter with the singing exercise. This is more unaccountable than any thing else I ever saw. The subject in a very happy state of mind would sing most melodiously, not from the mouth or nose, but entirely in the breast, the sounds issuing thence. Such music silenced every thing, and attracted the attention of all. It was most heavenly. None could ever be tired of hearing it. Doctor J. P. Campbell and myself were together at a meeting, and were attending to a pious lady thus exercised, and concluded it to be something surpassing any thing we had known in nature.

Thus have I given a brief account of the wonderful things that happened in the great excitement in the beginning of this century. That there were many eccentricities, and much fanaticism in this excitement, was acknowledged by its warmest advocates; indeed it would have been a wonder, if such things had not appeared, in the circumstances of that time. Yet the good effects were seen and acknowledged in every neighborhood, and among the different sects it silenced contention, and promoted unity for awhile; and these blessed effects would have continued, had not men put forth their unhallowed hands to hold up their tottering ark, mistaking it for the ark of God.

Question for Engagement

1. What criteria does Stone use throughout this excerpt to weigh the authenticity of the exercises?

5. Barton Stone's History of the Great Revival in the West (1827)

Excerpt from Stone, "History of the Christian Church, No. 1," Christian Messenger 1 (Feb. 1827): 74-79

Introduction

In his periodical, *Christian Messenger*, Barton Stone provided a history of the Christian Church. In this excerpt, Stone follows a typical pattern of revival narratives. That is, people had lost interest in religion, but a group of Christians prayed that God would revive religion. And, as Stone writes in the excerpt, God heard and "answered by fire." Stone reveals the way news of religious revival and exercises were communicated through letters and preachers, and he provides a brief account of revivals at his Concord and Cane Ridge congregations.

Excerpt

Towards the close of the eighteenth century, there was an unusual dearth in the professors of religion, throughout the western country, both among the preachers and the people. In the commencement of the present century, the more pious became seriously alarmed at the prevalence of vice and the declension of vital piety. They agreed to meet often in prayer to God to revive religion, which appeared ready to die. These meetings were frequent, and began to attract general attention. The humble Christians prayed fervently, and sang the praises of God with warm devotion. Their prayers reached the ears of the Lord; he answered by fire; for he poured out his spirit in a way almost miraculous. This powerful work was first experienced in Tennessee, and in the lower parts of this state, among the Presbyterians, in the summer or fall of 1800.

At this time I had gone to Virginia and North Carolina. From Carolina I was returning to Kentucky in company with Dr. Hall, who was going on a mission to Natchez and the low countries. Never shall I forget the events that transpired on our journey. We were met by a company returning from Tennessee, who had letters to Dr. Hall. We stopped in the woods. The Doctor began to read silently; but soon cried out aloud, and burst into a flood of tears. At first we were at a loss for the cause; but soon learned from the bearer of the letters, and from the letters themselves, that which equally affected us all. It was an account of a wonderful meeting at Shiloh in Tennessee—that many had been struck down as dead, and continued for hours apparently breathless, and afterwards rose, praising God for his saving mercy—that the saints were all alive—and sinners all around weeping and crying for mercy—and that multitudes were converted and rejoicing in God.

The work spread and progressed like fire in a dry stubble. The sparks, lighting in various parts of the field, would quickly raise as many blazes all around. So the Christians from various and distant parts met together; and returning home in the spirit and power of religion, they became preachers, successful preachers, in their neighborhoods, by simply stating what they had seen, heard, and felt; and so spake that many believed and turned to the Lord. . . .

In the spring of 1801, the Lord visited his people in the north of Kentucky. In Fleming, and in Concord, one of my congregations, the same strange and mighty works were seen and experienced. On the fourth Lord's day in May, we had an appointment for a communion at Concord. Various causes collected an unusual multitude of people together at this time,—between five and six thousands, of various sects, and many preachers. The house could not contain them, and we repaired to the woods. Worship commenced on Friday, and continued without intermission day and night, for four or five days. From this meeting, the flame spread all around, and increased till the ever-memorable meeting at Caneridge, in August following. Here an innumerable multitude collected, estimated at 25,000 souls. The meeting commenced on Friday, and continued six or seven days. It was truly a solemn scene to see the multitudes coming together, and the number of wagons and carriages bringing provisions and tents to stay on the ground; for it was found that no neighborhood could entertain and support the multitudes that came together. The members of the church and the neighbours brought their provisions to the encampment, for themselves and strangers. Long tables were spread with provisions, and all invited to eat. This was the beginning and introduction of camp meetings. During this time, night and day worship continued. Hundreds were lying as men slain in battle; many engaged in prayer for the distressed in every part of the camp; many in the woods around crying for mercy; many rejoicing aloud in songs of praise. In other parts many of the preachers of various names, were proclaiming the gospel of salvation. The number of converts could never be ascertained: it is thought to have been between 500 and 1000.

The doctrine preached by all was simple, and nearly the same. Free and full salvation to every creature was proclaimed. All urged faith in the gospel, and obedience to it, as the way of life. All appeared deeply impressed with the ruined state of sinners, and were anxious for their salvation. The spirit of partyism, and party distinctions, were apparently forgotten. The doctrines of former controversy were not named; no mention was made of eternal unconditional election, reprobation, or fatality. The spirit of love, peace, and union, were revived. You might have seen the various sects engaged in the same spirit, praying, praising, and communing together, and the preachers in the lead. Happy days! joyful seasons of refreshment from the presence of the Lord! This work from this period spread throughout the western country. . . .

Questions for Engagement

1. What was the fruit of the revival as described by Stone?

2. What are the key methods and means of spreading revival, according to Stone's narrative?

6. Barton Stone Supports Revivals of Religion (1831)

Excerpt from Stone, "Revivals of Religion," *Christian Messenger* 5 (Aug. 1831): 164–67

Introduction

As reports of revivals in the East in 1831 made their way to Barton Stone, he recollected fondly the Great Revival in the West and the many positive effects it had on people and Christianity. In this excerpt, Stone provides his reasons for believing Christians should support revivals.

Excerpt

While I hear daily of the great revivals in many parts of the East, my mind with a mournful pleasure reverts to the great revival of the West 30 years ago, and which continued for several years, and spread far and wide. To give a full history of it would be impossible. Often I have gazed with inexpressible emotions at the gathering crowds hurrying to the place of worship. All clothed with solemnity—many wetting their paths with tears—and thousands anxious to find the way of life—many sunk under the burden of sin, and little groups around pointing to them the hope of Israel, and uniting their solemn prayers for their salvation. Many praising God aloud for delivering grace, and cheerfully uniting with the church of God. Thousands silently hanging on the lips of the preacher, who in the warm, loving spirit of his Lord, was ministering to them the word of reconciliation. I then saw, and yet acknowledge some imperfection, some eccentricities or aberrations from what I thought right, among the vast multitudes assembled. But I remembered they were but men, and that I could not reasonably expect to find perfection in such multitudes of imperfect beings. The good so far exceeded the evil, the latter almost disappeared. I saw the religion of Jesus more clearly exhibited in the lives of Christians then, than I had ever seen before or since to the same extent. The preachers were revived. I saw them filled with the Holy Spirit of their Lord, addressing the multitudes, not in Icebergh style, nor according to the studied rules of rhetoric and oratory; but in the language and spirit of heaven. Impressed with the worth of souls—of unconverted souls, exposed to everlasting punishment—feeling their awful responsibility to God; and feeling the force of divine truth, and the power of religion, in their own souls, they spoke with earnestness, as dying men to dying men. . . . Through many difficulties, they labored night and day, privately and publicly, from house to house, from neighborhood to neighborhood, preaching the word of salvation to all, not for filthy lucre, but of a ready mind; they labored to save souls, and to establish them in the faith and hope of the gospel,—they, feeling the spirit of love, peace and union, endeavored to promote and cultivate these essentials of religion, wherever they could.

I saw the congregations revived. The saints of every name mingling together, and together offering their sacrifices of prayer and praise in the fire of love to their common Father and Redeemer, and together surrounding the table of their Lord. How affecting! to see parents then weeping over their unconverted children, and praying fervently for them—to see brothers and sisters engaged in the same work for their brothers and [165] sisters—neighbor for neighbor—friends for their friends and enemies. All, old and young, even small children engaged in the same work, not only at the place of worship, but at home and abroad. . . .

I saw sinners every where, of every age and sex, rich and poor, bond and free, old and young, weeping, praying, and converting to God—I saw enemies become friends, and sweetly united in the bonds of love—I saw brotherly kindness, meekness, gentleness, obedience, all the divine graces, growing and abounding among the saints of God. The Bible was read with intense desire to find the truth. This, this I call a revival. This I call the work of God. . . .

The great obstruction to this revival was the spirit of sectarianism, which like a restless demon, infected and destroyed the glorious work, wherever it came. Never can this spirit, and the spirit of Christ amalgamate. As much opposed as darkness and light—as fire and water, are they.

Shall we oppose revivals because we discover in them much enthusiasm, mismanagement, and unscriptural means employed by those engaged in them? If we do, we may also oppose every good, not perfect, or to which is attached any imperfection. The imperfection should be opposed, but in the meekness and gentleness of Christ; but great care should be taken that while rooting out the tares, we do not root out the wheat.

Shall we oppose a revival, because we think the conductors of it are ignorant of what we may deem the most important doctrine of the gospel? If this be our privilege, it is also the privilege of all; every party will reject of course every revival not their own. If genuine religion be the fruit of such revivals, we dare not reject without incurring the divine displeasure.

I have read in an Eastern paper of the character of the revivals in one section of that country. It states that Christians of all denominations lovingly united in worship, even in the breaking of bread at the Lord's table. In such a work I will rejoice. Yet I have my fears that the demon of partyism will check and destroy it. Yet Christianity will prevail so far as to have enlisted under her banners many, who cannot and will not be drawn into the vortex of sectarianism, and who will remain free, and preach reformation to the sects in bondage.

Questions for Engagement

1. What are Stone's main reasons for believing that Christians should support revivals?

2. What was the "great obstruction" to the revival?

7. Peter Cartwright on the Cane Ridge Revival and the Stone Campbell Movement (1857)

Excerpt from Cartwright, *Autobiography of Peter Cartwright*, 30–33.

Introduction

This excerpt from famous Methodist revivalist Peter Cartwright's autobiography is of interest not for the accuracy of its details (some facts such as the duration of the Cane Ridge revival are wrong) but for its illustration of how some Christian leaders viewed Cane Ridge and reasons some rejected the Stone-Campbell "plea" for Christian unity based upon restoration of the beliefs and practices of the New Testament church.

Excerpt

Somewhere between 1800 and 1801, in the upper part of Kentucky, at a memorable place called "Cane Ridge," there was appointed a sacramental meeting by some of the Presbyterian ministers, at which meeting, seemingly unexpected by ministers or people, the mighty power of God was displayed in a very extraordinary manner; many were moved to tears, and bitter and loud crying for mercy. The meeting was protracted for weeks. Ministers of almost all denominations flocked in from far and near. The meeting was kept up by night and day. Thousands heard of the mighty work, and came on foot, on horseback, in carriages and wagons. It was supposed that there were in attendance at times during the meeting from twelve to twenty-five thousand people. Hundreds fell prostrate under the mighty power of God, as men slain in battle. Stands were erected in the woods from which preachers of different Churches proclaimed repentance toward God and faith in our Lord Jesus Christ, and it was supposed, by eye and ear witnesses, that between one and two thousand souls were happily and powerfully converted to God during the meeting. It was not unusual for one, two, three, and four to seven preachers to be addressing the listening thousands at the same time from the different stands erected for the purpose. The heavenly fire spread in almost every direction. It was said, by truthful witnesses, that at times more than one thousand persons broke out into loud shouting all at once, and that the shouts could be heard for miles around.

From this camp-meeting, for so it ought to be called, the news spread through all the Churches, and through all the land, and it excited great wonder and surprise; but it kindled a religious flame that spread all over Kentucky and through many other states. And I may here be permitted to say, that this was the first camp-meeting ever held in the United States, and here our camp-meetings took their rise.

As Presbyterian, Methodist, and Baptist ministers all united in the blessed work at this meeting, when they returned home to their different congregations, and carried the news of this mighty work, the revival spread rapidly throughout the land; but many of the ministers and members of the synod of Kentucky thought it all disorder, and tried to stop the work. They called their preachers who were engaged in the revival to account, and censured and silenced them. These ministers then rose up and unitedly renounced the jurisdiction of the Presbyterian Church, organized a Church of their own, and dubbed it with the name of *Christian*. Here was the origin of what was called the *New Lights*. They renounced the Westminster Confession of Faith, and all Church discipline, and professed to take the New Testament for their Church discipline. They established no standard of doctrine; every one was to take the New Testament, read it, and abide his own construction of it. Marshall, M'Namar, Dunlevy, Stone, Huston, and others, were the chief leaders in this *trash trap*. Soon a diversity of opinion sprang up, and they got into a Babel confusion. Some preached Arian, some Socinian, and some Universalist doctrines; so that in a few years you could not tell what was *harped* or what was *danced*. They adopted the mode of immersion, the water-god of all exclusive errorists; and directly there was a mighty controversy about the way to heaven, whether it was by water or by dry land. . . .

Soon the Shaker priests came along, and off went M'Namar, Dunlevy, and Huston, into that foolish error. Marshall and others retraced their steps. B. W. Stone stuck to his New Lightism, and fought many bloodless battles, till he grew old and feeble, and the mighty Alexander Campbell, the *great*, arose and poured such floods of regenerating water about the old man's cranium, that he formed a union with this giant errorist, and finally died, not much lamented out of the circle of a few friends. And this is the way with all the New Lights, in the government, morals, and discipline of the Church.

This Christian, or New Light Church, is a feeble and scattered people, though there are some good Christians among them. I suppose since the day of Pentecost, there was hardly ever a greater revival of religion than at Cane Ridge; and if there had been steady, Christian ministers, settled in Gospel doctrine and Church discipline, thousands might have been saved to the Church that wandered off in the mazes of vain, speculative divinity, and finally made shipwreck of the faith, fell back, turned infidel, and lost their religion and their souls forever. But evidently a new impetus was given to the work of God, and many, very many, will have cause to bless God forever for this revival of religion throughout the length and breadth of our Zion.

Questions for Engagement

1. How does Cartwright view Cane Ridge?

2. How does he view the Stone and Campbell movements when writing in 1856?

3. What SCM beliefs or practices does Cartwright clearly or subtly reject?

References

Allen, Leonard. *Distant Voices: Discovering a Forgotten Past for a Changing Church*. Abilene, TX: ACU Press, 1993.

———. *Poured Out: The Spirit of God Empowering the Mission of God*. Abilene, TX: ACU Press, 2018.

———. *Things Unseen: Churches of Christ in (and after) the Modern Age*. Abilene, TX: Leafwood Publishers, 2004.

Allen, Leonard, and Danny Swick. *Participating in God's Life: Two Crossroads for Churches of Christ*. Abilene, TX: Leafwood Publishers, 2003.

Allen, Thomas M. "Letters on Revivals." *Christian Messenger* 2 (June 1828): 189–91.

———. "REVIVALS." *Christian Messenger* 2 (Apr. 1828): 140–41.

Armenius, Theophilus. "Account of the Rise and Progress of the Work of God in the Western Country, No. III." *Methodist Magazine* 2 (July 1819): 272.

Asbury, Francis. *The Journal of the Rev. Francis Asbury, Bishop of the Methodist Episcopal Church*. 3 vols. New York: Lane & Scott, 1852.

Bevins, Winfield. "The Historical Development of Wesley's Doctrine of the Spirit." *Wesleyan Theological Journal* 41 (Fall 2006): 161–81.

Boles, John B. *The Great Revival: Beginnings of the Bible Belt.* Lexington: University Press of Kentucky, 1996.

Braude, Amy. *Sisters and Saints: Women and American Religion.* Oxford: Oxford University Press, 2008.

Brekus, Catherine A. *Strangers and Pilgrims: Female Preaching in America, 1740–1845.* Chapel Hill: University of North Carolina Press, 1998.

Bruce, Dickson D., Jr. "Camp Meetings." In *Encyclopedia of Religion in America*, edited by Charles H. Lippy and Peter W. Williams, 1:347–52. Washington, DC: CQ Press, 2010.

Caldwell, Finis Jay, Jr. *Dr. David Caldwell: An 18th Century Flame for Christ.* Lubbock, TX: Mumbo Jumbo Multimedia, 2008.

Campbell, Alexander. "An Address to the Readers of the Christian Baptist. No. IV." *Christian Baptist* 1 (Mar. 1824): 148.

———. "Christendom in Its Dotage." *Millennial Harbinger* (Aug. 1834): 371–75.

———. "The Confirmation of the Testimony." *Millennial Harbinger* (Jan. 1830): 8–14.

———. "Dialogue on the Holy Spirit—Part 1." *Millennial Harbinger* (July 1831): 288–97.

———. "Dialogue on the Holy Spirit—Part 2." *Millennial Harbinger* (Aug. 1831): 363–69.

———. "Incidents on a Tour to Nashville, TN. No. 1." *Millennial Harbinger* (Dec. 1830): 553–60.

———. "Kingdom of the Clergy." *Christian Baptist* 1 (Sep. 1823): 49–56

———. "Letter to William Jones, No. VI." *Millennial Harbinger* (Aug. 1835): 350–57.

———. "Mr. Lynd on the Influence of the Holy Spirit." *Millennial Harbinger* (Sep. 1837): 410.

———. "Prayer—No. 1." *Millennial Harbinger* (Oct. 1831): 471.

———. "Reply on Union, Communion, and the Name Christian." *Millennial Harbinger* (Sep. 1831): 389–96.

———. "Reply to Mr. Waterman." *Millennial Harbinger* (June 1834): 250–52.

Campbell, Thomas. "An Address to All Our Christian Brethren: Upon the Necessity and Importance of the Actual Enjoyment of Our Holy Religion." *Millennial Harbinger* (May 1844): 199.

Carroll, Bret E. *The Routledge Historical Atlas of Religion in America.* New York: Routledge, 2000.

Cartwright, Peter. *Autobiography of Peter Cartwright*, edited by Charles L. Wallis. New York: Abingdon, 1956.

Clary, Glen J. "Holy Communion and Revivalism in the First Great Awakening." *The Confessional Presbyterian* 11 (2015): 100–111.

Cohen, Charles L. "Great Awakening." In *Dictionary of American History*, edited by Stanley I. Kutler. 3rd ed. 4:38. New York: Charles Scribner's Sons, 2003.

Conkin, Paul Keith. *Cane Ridge: America's Pentecost.* Madison: University of Wisconsin Press, 1990.

Davies, Samuel. *Important Subjects, by the Revered Samuel Davies, A.M., President of the College of New-Jersey*, edited by Albert Barnes. New York: Dayton and Saxton, 1841.

Douglass, Frederick. "What, to the Slave, Is the Fourth of July?" In *Lift Every Voice: African American Oratory, 1787–1900*, edited by Philip S. Foner and Robert James Branham, 246–68. Tuscaloosa: University of Alabama Press, 1998 [1852].

Dunnavant, Anthony L. *Cane Ridge in Context: Perspectives on Barton W. Stone and the Revival.* Disciples of Christ Historical Society, 1992.

Edwards, Jonathan. *Religious Affections.* New Haven, CT: Yale University Press, 1959.

Fawcett, Arthur. *The Cambuslang Revival: The Scottish Evangelical Revival of the Eighteenth Century.* Edinburgh: Banner of Truth Trust, 1971.

Fikes, Jason. "From Sacramental Season to Observance on the Lord's Day: Learning from Barton Stone's Communion Journey." *Christian Studies* 30 (2018): 71–84.

Garrison, William Lloyd. "Address to the People of the United States on Slavery." *Christian Messenger* 9 (Apr. 1835): 82–88.

Gaustad, Edwin Scott, Philip L. Barlow, and Richard W. Dishno. *New Historical Atlas of Religion in America*. 3rd ed. New York: Oxford University Press, 2001.

Goodnight, Cloyd, and Dwight Stevenson. *Home to Bethphage: The Life of Robert Richardson*. St. Louis: Christian Board of Publication, 1949.

Gorman, James L. *Among the Early Evangelicals: Transatlantic Origins of the Stone-Campbell Movement*. Abilene, TX: ACU Press, 2017.

———. "Evangelical Revivalism and Race Relations in the Early National Era." In *Slavery's Long Shadow: Race and Reconciliation in American Christianity*, edited by James L. Gorman, Jeff W. Childers, and Mark Hamilton, 21–38. Grand Rapids: Eerdmans, 2019.

Gregg, John, and James Gregg. "An Apology for Withdrawing from the Methodist Episcopal Church." *Christian Messenger* 1 (Dec. 1826): 37–43.

Haggard, Rice. *An Address to the Different Religious Societies on the Sacred Import of the Christian Name*. Lexington: Joseph Charles, 1804.

Hall, B. F. "The Proud Preacher: The Autobiography of B. F. Hall." Unpublished manuscript, n.d. Center for Restoration Studies, Abilene Christian University.

Harding, James. "Atlanta—God's Providence—The Holy Spirit." *Christian Leader and the Way* 20 (June 19, 1906): 9.

———. "God's Churches versus Man's Societies, No. II." *Christian Leader and the Way* 19 (Jan. 1905): 8.

———. "How Does God Help His People?" *Christian Leader and the Way* 20 (Feb. 1906): 9.

Hatch, Nathan O. *The Democratization of American Christianity*. New Haven: Yale University Press, 1989.

Hicks, John Mark, and Bobby Valentine. *Kingdom Come: Embracing the Spiritual Legacy of David Lipscomb and James Harding*. Abilene, TX: Leafwood Publishers, 2006.

Hughes, Richard T. "The Apocalyptic Origins of Churches of Christ and the Triumph of Modernism." *Religion and American Culture* 2 (1992): 181–214.

———. "'The Politics of the Day' and 'The Politics of Heaven': The Apocalyptic Orientation of Barton W. Stone." In *Resisting Babel: Allegiance to God and the Problem of Government*, edited by John Mark Hicks, 15–35. Abilene, TX: ACU Press, 2020.

———. *Reviving the Ancient Faith: The Story of Churches of Christ in America*. Abilene, TX: ACU Press, 2008 [1996].

Kidd, Thomas S. *The Great Awakening: The Roots of Evangelical Christianity in Colonial America*. New Haven: Yale University Press, 2007.

Latrobe, Benjamin H. "Plan of the Camp, August 8, 1809." In *Journal of Benjamin Latrobe* (Aug. 23, 1806–Aug. 8, 1809). Latrobe Papers, Manuscript Department. Maryland Historical Society, Baltimore. www.loc.gov/exhibits/religion/vc006753.jpg.

Lee, Jarena. *Religious Experience and Journal of Mrs. Jarena Lee, Giving an Account of Her Call to Preach the Gospel*. Philadelphia: Published for the author, 1849.

M'Corkle, James. "Letter from James M'Corkle Dated January 8, 1802, Documenting a Revival in Randolph, North Carolina." In *A Narrative of a Most Extraordinary Work of Religion in North Carolina by the Rev. James Hall. Also a Collection of Interesting Letters from the Rev. James M'Corkle*, edited by James Hall and James M'Corkle. Philadelphia: William Woodward, 1802.

M'Gready, James. *The Posthumous Works of the Reverend and Pious James M'Gready*, edited by James Smith. 2 vols. Nashville: Printed by Lowry and Smith, 1831 and 1833.

Mahaffey, Jerome Dean. *The Accidental Revolutionary: George Whitefield and the Creation of America*. Waco: Baylor University Press, 2011.

McClymond, Michael J. "Christian Revival and Renewal Movements." In *The Wiley-Blackwell Companion to World Christianity*, edited by Lamin Sanneh and Michael J. McClymond, 244–62. Chichester: Wiley-Blackwell, 2016.

McNemar, Richard. *The Kentucky Revival, or, A Short History of the Late Extraordinary Out-Pouring of the Spirit of God, in the Western States of America*. Cincinnati: John W. Browne, 1807.

Moore, Joseph S., and Robert M. Calhoon. "Evangelicals: Nineteenth Century." In *Encyclopedia of Religion in America*, edited by Charles H. Lippy and Peter W. Williams. Washington, DC: CQ Press, 2010.

Olson, Roger. "A Pentecost Sermon: The Holy Spirit." *Roger E. Olson: My Evangelical Arminian Theological Musings* (Patheos blog). May 2016. www.patheos.com/blogs/rogereolson/2016/05/a-pentecost-sermon-the-holy-spirit/.

Opie, John. "James McGready: Theologian of Frontier Revivalism." *Church History* 34 (1965): 445–56.

Price, Barton. "Great Awakening(s)." In *Encyclopedia of Religion in America*, edited by Charles H. Lippy and Peter W. Williams. Washington, DC: CQ Press, 2010.

Rice, David. *A Sermon on the Present Revival of Religion, etc. in This Country; Preached at the Opening of the Kentucky Synod*. Lexington: Printed by Joseph Charles, 1803.

Richardson, Robert. "Faith vs Philosophy—No 5." *Millennial Harbinger* (1857): 328–36.

Roberts, R. L. "Early Tennessee and Kentucky Preachers." Transcribed by Erma Jean Loveland. https://webfiles.acu.edu/departments/Library/HR/restmov_nov11/www.mun.ca/rels/restmov/texts/resources/TNKY.htm.

Roberts, R. L., and J. W. Roberts. "Like Fire in Dry Stubble—The Stone Movement, 1804–1832 (Part I)." *Restoration Quarterly* 7 (1963): 148–58.

———. "Like Fire in Dry Stubble (Part II)." *Restoration Quarterly* 9 (1965): 26–40.

Rogers, John. "The Church of Christ at Concord, to the Elders and Brethren Assembled in Conference at Caneridge, Sendeth Christian Salutation." *Christian Messenger* 4 (Oct. 1830): 257–58.

Rogers, John Richard, and Barton Warren Stone. "A Short History of the Life of Barton W. Stone: Written by Himself, Designed

Principally for His Children and Christian Friends." In *The Cane Ridge Meeting-House*, edited by William Rogers. 2nd ed. Cincinnati: The Standard Publishing Company, 1910.

Schmidt, Leigh Eric. *Holy Fairs: Scotland and the Making of American Revivalism*. 2nd ed. Grand Rapids: Eerdmans, 2001.

———. "'A Practical Remembrance': Cane Ridge in Historical Memory." *Discipliana* 61 (Summer 2001): 35–48.

Scott, John Thomas. "James McGready: Son of Thunder, Father of the Great Revival." PhD diss., Williamsburg, VA, The College of William and Mary, 1991.

Shiels, Richard D. "America's Pentecost." *Cross Currents* 42 (Spring 1992): 90–100.

Smith, Benjamin L. *Alexander Campbell*. St. Louis: Bethany Press, 1930.

Smith, Thomas. "To the Editor of the Christian Messenger." *Christian Messenger* 1 (Sep. 1827): 249–51.

Stone, Barton Warren. "Christian Expositor." *Christian Messenger* 12 (July 1842): 272–74.

———. *The Biography of Eld. Barton Warren Stone, Written by Himself; with Additions and Reflections*, edited by John Rogers. Cincinnati: J. A. & U. P. James, 1847.

———. "Christian Union, Lecture III." *Christian Messenger* 11 (May 1841): 312–17.

———. "The Conference in Terra Confusa." *Christian Messenger* 9 (July 1835): 152–56.

———. "History of the Christian Church. No. I." *Christian Messenger* 1 (Feb. 1827): 74–79.

———. "An Interview between an Old and Young Preacher." *Christian Messenger* 14 (Dec. 1844): 225–30.

———. "Letter to Walter Scott." *Christian Messenger* 10 (1836): 13–14.

———. "Objections to Christian Union Calmly Considered." *Christian Messenger* 1 (Dec. 1826): 27.

———. "On Prayer." *Christian Messenger* 1 (Aug. 1827): 235–37.

———. "Query." *Christian Messenger* 4 (Sep. 1830): 228–29.

———. "Reflections of Old Age." *Christian Messenger* 13 (Aug. 1843): 123–26.

———. *A Reply to John P. Campbell's Strictures on Atonement.* Lexington: Joseph Charles, 1805.

———. "Reply to T. P. Ware." *Christian Messenger* 14 (Oct. 1844): 166–71.

———. "Retrospect." *Christian Messenger* 7 (Oct. 1833): 314–16.

———. "Revivals of Religion." *Christian Messenger* 5 (July 1831): 164–67.

———. "A Short History of the Life of Barton W. Stone Written by Himself." In *Voices from Cane Ridge*, edited by Rhodes Thompson. St. Louis: Bethany Press, 1954.

———. "To the Editors of the Baptist Recorder." *Christian Messenger* 1 (Aug. 1827): 221–25.

———. "Union." *Christian Messenger* 5 (Aug. 1831): 180–85.

Stone, Barton Warren, Robert Marshall, John Dunlavy, Richard M'Nemar, and John Thompson. *An Apology for Renouncing the Jurisdiction of the Synod of Kentucky*. In *The Biography of Eld. Barton Warren Stone*, edited by John Rogers. Cincinnati: J. A. & U. P. James, 1847.

Tennent, Gilbert. "The Danger of an Unconverted Ministry (1740)." In *The Great Awakening: Documents on the Revival of Religion, 1740-1745*, edited by Richard L. Bushman, 87–93. Chapel Hill: University of North Carolina Press, 1989.

Thomas, Joseph. *The Travels and Gospel Labors of Joseph Thomas.* Winchester, VA: Jonathan Foster, 1812.

Turner, Frederick Jackson. "The Significance of the Frontier in American History." In *The Frontier in American History*, 1–38. New York: Henry Holt and Company, 1921.

Valentine, Robert P., Jr. "Robertson Lafayette Whiteside: Systematic Theologian for the Churches of Christ." Unpublished manuscript, Harding University Graduate School of Religion, 2001.

Weber, Timothy P. *Living in the Shadow of the Second Coming: American Premillennialism, 1875–1925*. New York: Oxford University Press, 1979.

Wesley, John. *Fifty-Three Sermons*, edited by Edward H. Sugden. Nashville: Abingdon Press, 1984.

West, William Garrett. *Barton Warren Stone: Early American Advocate of Christian Unity*. Nashville: The Disciples of Christ Historical Society, 1954.

Whitefield, George. *The Nature and Necessity of Our New Birth in Christ Jesus, in Order to Salvation: A Sermon Preached in the Church of St. Mary Radcliffe, in Bristol*. 2nd ed. London: Printed for C. Rivington in St. Paul's Church-yard, 1737.

Williams, D. Newell. *Barton Stone: A Spiritual Biography*. St. Louis: Chalice Press, 2000.

———. "From Trusting Congress to Renouncing Human Governments: The Millennial Odyssey of Barton Stone." *Discipliana* 61 (2001): 67–81.

———. "Our Unity in Christ: From Cane Ridge to Kansas City." *Lexington Theological Journal* 46 (2016): 43–51.

———. "Pursuit of Justice: The Antislavery Pilgrimage of Barton W. Stone." *Encounter* 62 (2001): 1–23.

Woodward, William W., ed. *Surprising Accounts of the Revival of Religion, in the United States of America, in Different Parts of the World, and among Different Denominations of Christians*. Philadelphia: William W. Woodward, 1802. https://webfiles.acu.edu/departments/Library/HR/restmov_nov11/www.mun.ca/rels/restmov/texts/accounts/accounts.html.

Contributors

Leonard Allen serves as dean of the College of Bible and Ministry at Lipscomb University in Nashville. He taught theology, ethics, and philosophy for many years at Abilene Christian University, Biola University, Fuller Theological Seminary, and John Brown University. He has spoken widely on college campuses and in churches over the past thirty-five years on biblical, historical, and theological themes. He is the author of numerous books, including *The Cruciform Church: Becoming a Cross-Shaped People in a Secular World*, *Distant Voices: Discovering a Forgotten Past for a Changing Church*, *Things Unseen: Churches of Christ in (and after) the Modern Age*, and most recently, *Poured Out: The Spirit of God Empowering the Mission of God*.

Carisse Mickey Berryhill serves as special collections librarian at Abilene Christian University's Brown Library. Before coming to ACU, she was associate librarian at Harding School of Theology in Memphis, Tennessee (1992–2004), and professor of English at Lubbock Christian University (1975–1992). Berryhill holds advanced degrees in English, library science, and church history.

She does research in rhetoric in the Stone-Campbell movement and its eighteenth-century Scottish roots. She has received ACU's Faculty Service Award, and Pepperdine University's Distinguished Christian Service Award for her efforts the in preservation of Stone-Campbell history. She currently serves as chair of the corporation board of *Restoration Quarterly*.

James Gorman serves as professor of history at Johnson University in Knoxville, Tennessee. His teaching, research, and writing engages the history of Christianity, Stone-Campbell movement history, race and Christianity, and the history of Bible interpretation. He authored *Among the Early Evangelicals: The Transatlantic Origins of the Stone-Campbell Movement* and coedited *Slavery's Long Shadow: Race and Reconciliation in American Christianity*. He serves as assistant editor of *Stone-Campbell Journal* and coordinates the History and Theology of the *Stone-Campbell Movement* study group at the annual *Stone-Campbell Journal* Conference.

John Mark Hicks has taught systematic and historical theology for thirty-eight years in institutions of higher learning among Churches of Christ. He has taught at Alabama Christian School of Religion (now Amridge), Magnolia Bible College, and Harding School of Theology. He currently serves as professor of Theology in the Hazelip School of Theology, Lipscomb University, Nashville. He has published twenty books, including *Kingdom Come: Embracing the Legacy of David Lipscomb and James Harding* (with Bobby Valentine), *Come to the Table: Revisioning the Lord's Supper*, *Resisting Babel: Allegiance to God and the Problem of Government* (editor), and *Searching for the Pattern: My Journey in Interpreting the Bible*.

Richard Hughes has worked at the intersection of religion and American culture over the course of a forty-nine-year career, specializing in the history of Churches of Christ, religion and American identity; religion and race in America; religion and American higher education; and the role of Christian primitivism in American life. His eighteen published books include *Reviving the Ancient Faith: The Story of Churches of Christ in America* and *Myths America Lives By: White Supremacy and the Stories That Give Us Meaning* (revised edition). He has taught at Pepperdine University, Abilene Christian University, and Messiah College, and currently serves as scholar-in-residence in the College of Bible and Ministry at Lipscomb University.